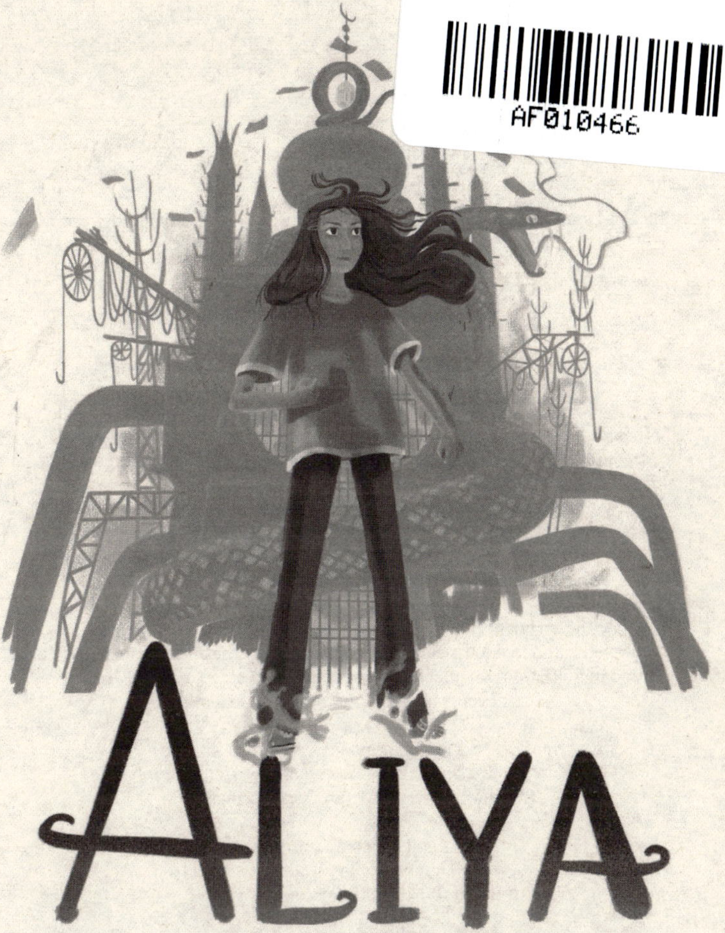

ALIYA AND THE SHOP OF SECOND CHANCES

Laila Rifaat

Chicken House

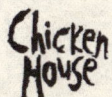

2 Palmer Street, Frome,
Somerset BA11 1DS
www.chickenhousebooks.com

First published in the UK in 2025
Chicken House
2 Palmer Street
Frome, Somerset BA11 1DS
United Kingdom
www.chickenhousebooks.com

Chicken House/Scholastic Ireland, 89E Lagan Road, Dublin Industrial Estate,
Glasnevin, Dublin D11 HP5F, Republic of Ireland

Text © Laila Rifaat 2025
Illustration © Gaia Alessi 2025

The moral rights of the author and illustrator have been asserted.

All rights reserved.
No part of this publication may be reproduced, transmitted, downloaded,
decompiled, reverse engineered, used to train any artificial intelligence
technologies, or stored in or introduced into any information storage and
retrieval system, in any form or by any means, whether electronic or mechanical,
now known or hereafter invented, without the express written permission
of the publisher. Subject to EU law the publisher expressly reserves this
work from the text and data mining exception.

This book is a work of fiction. Names, characters, businesses, organizations,
places, events and incidents are either the product of the author's imagination
or used in a fictitious manner. Any resemblance to actual persons, living or
dead, events or locales is purely coincidental.

For safety or quality concerns:
UK: www.chickenhousebooks.com/productinformation
EU: www.scholastic.ie/productinformation

Cover design by Helen Crawford-White
Typeset by Dorchester Typesetting Group Ltd
Printed in the UK by Clays, Elcograf S.p.A

1 3 5 7 9 10 8 6 4 2

A CIP catalogue record for this book is available from the British Library.

PB ISBN 978-1-915026-37-8
eISBN 978-1-915947-79-6

To the Stelzer family,
for always keeping their door open

Chapter 1
PORTALS AND PREMONITIONS

Aliya Sultan stretched out her trembling hands and took a deep breath. She could feel her palms light up, beginning to radiate and glow with colour: blue, silver and pink. The travel key felt heavy in her hands as she carefully inserted it into the lock of the wooden door that stood before her in the middle of the room. But just before turning it, she hesitated.

'All right,' said her mentor, Professor Nigm, who stood next to her. His voice was as soft as the smoke from his silver pipe. 'Clear your mind and focus. Quickly now, before Simi gets impatient.'

Aliya glanced down at the key, alight with the same colour as her palms.

Simi. She was not just a time key, but her *nadim*. In this shape, she was the tool that helped Aliya open portals, and even create them. In her other form, as a beautiful hoopoe bird, she was a companion. All travellers had keys, but only locksmiths like Aliya had keys like this, which were *extra*.

Aliya's stomach grumbled and she squeezed Simi a little too hard.

Relax, she thought. *I'm still learning. It's OK. They were all making mistakes like these at the beginning.*

'They' referred to the older and more experienced locksmith apprentices whom Aliya could see passing by outside the workshop, elegant in their crisp uniforms. She would just wait until they were out of sight, she decided. But now they were stopping to watch her! *Why does the Smithy have such big windows everywhere?*

The key twitched in her hand. Simi was getting impatient. A moment or two longer and she would turn back into a bird and fly off, then circle back and target Aliya with luminous droppings – something the nadim did as revenge every time Aliya grabbed her too hard.

'Don't mind them,' Professor Nigm said, pointing his pipe shaft at the students. 'You've got just as much right to be here.'

Aliya glanced up at him for reassurance. Since she had become his apprentice a year before, they hadn't exactly grown close. Professor Nigm was much too forbidding for that. But she trusted him. There was something reassuring about his stern face with its aquiline nose, and his white turban that reminded her of an onion. Puffing on his own nadim, a thin silver pipe, he released a cloud of lilac smoke at her. Lavender. For calming her nerves.

Aliya tried to ignore the gleeful faces on the other side of the window. She raised her hands again and felt Simi stirring in anticipation. Despite being in her second year in the time-travel world, she was still the youngest of the locksmith apprentices. The Smithy didn't necessarily take on new students every year, so the others were all older and more experienced, something they wouldn't let her forget.

Now turn the key slowly, she thought. *And think of the practice room in Casablanca.* She pictured the red velvet armchair that stood in a similar workshop, but in a sister hub in Morocco, one that locksmith apprentices opened portals to for practice. The red armchair was a good prop – an item to help students focus.

Aliya turned her key. A soft light pulsed out from under the door and through the keyhole, the telltale sign that a portal had been opened. Pulling the door open, she held her breath . . . but no.

This was not the sister hub in Casablanca. With horror, she realized she was looking in at Uncle Hamdy, the stout Egyptian man who ran the food joint on the corner of her old street back in Cairo. Hamdy sat, frozen, tea glass raised halfway to his lips, staring at her. Aliya and Geddo had been getting their koshary from Uncle Hamdy's for as long as she could remember. The mix of rice, lentils and macaroni with spicy red sauce and crisp fried onions had been their favourite Friday meal.

A quick glance around told Aliya that she was staring out at him from a portal that, on his side, was a refrigerator. Whatever thoughts Uncle Hamdy was forming about her appearing in his fridge were cut short by the mist of lotus spray that Professor Nigm expertly aimed at his face. One puff would make him forget he'd ever seen them.

Taking Simi out of Aliya's hands, Nigm performed a reverse turn of the key blade and the portal closed. Outside the workshop window, the older apprentices were romping about. Were they laughing at her? She wasn't sure. She imagined Uncle Hamdy blinking in surprise, then looking down at his tea glass, trying to regain his bearings.

The door behind them opened and an older student hurried in, clutching a sleek tablet.

'I'm really sorry,' Aliya said quickly, to intercept the interruption. 'Can I have another go?'

But Nigm's attention had turned to the student, a tall Mamluk youth called Omar Sadik.

'A message, sir.' Omar stuck the tablet into Nigm's hands. 'It's urgent.'

The professor glanced at the screen, his face darkening.

'What is it?' Aliya asked. 'Is something wrong?'

'We'll try again next time,' Nigm mumbled, his thoughts elsewhere. Aliya looked expectantly at the tablet, hoping he would share the news. But of course he wasn't going to tell her what was the matter. He was kind in his own way, and wise, possibly even quite fond of her, but she was just one of the myriad responsibilities he had as elder locksmith.

'I've got to go.' He looked up at her. 'Maybe . . . have breakfast before our next session?'

'Ouch!' Omar grinned. 'You had a bit of a rumbly tummy?'

Aliya felt her cheeks heat up. She had opened two portals that morning, both to street-food vendors, because she'd been hungry. But that was not all. She was starting to gain a reputation for portal-opening blunders. Last week, she'd opened a portal into the ladies' toilet at Grand Central Station (she had needed a wee), and then into the thick of a Mongol raid on Baghdad (what she had been reading about for history class). That exercise had gone particularly wrong. Openings to other times always had to be made in discreet places, to out-of-the-way storage cupboards or dusty cellars in derelict buildings, so that the time-travellers could sneak into a new time undetected. The mishap had earnt her a week's polishing duty in the key nursery, where she had been bossed around by a grump – a small hamster-like creature with a whole lot of attitude.

Her mistakes were never dangerous, though. Professor Nigm always had the shield on when Aliya was practising, a safety device that ensured that nothing could enter through the portal into the Smithy.

'Why don't you join the others for the rest of the lesson?' Professor Nigm said. A ringlet of smoke, deep blue now, coiled around her shoulders for a moment before dissolving. Nigm's way of saying goodbye.

'Yalla,' Omar said when Aliya made no move to follow them out of the workshop. 'You know you're not allowed in here alone.'

'I *know*,' she shot back. 'I'm just gonna get my things.'

'We'll be in the carpet nursery.'

Omar gave her an amused look before turning and following Nigm towards the exit.

She returned his smile with a grimace. She was the youngest apprentice, the mascot, the joke . . .

Aliya headed towards the other end of the workshop where her satchel lay on a table. Above her, Simi had changed back to bird form and was whistling in a loop around the room, her luminous crest raised. Aliya gazed up at her. The nadim had always been a strange creature. Maybe because she had picked her out of the most dangerous travel key in the Infinitum. Simi had once been part of the Darkling – the key that belonged to the magician Dorian Darke. She had been the grain of Sublime energy that formed the eye of his snake-shaped key. But after Aliya had stolen and released her from his magic, Simi had metamorphosed into her present form and chosen to become her companion.

Yes, they were companions of a sort. Even so, Aliya often felt lost in the nadim's presence. Last year, before she had taken her final winged shape, Simi had given her all kinds of trouble with her shapeshifting, raspberry-blowing, setting-fire-to-things habits. Now, after a period of calm, she had begun to grow . . . restless, was that it? Some days, the nadim lounged about for hours, uninterested in the apprentice stuff they were supposed to be studying, like vitalizing time-travel devices or opening portals. At other times, she was fretful and unpredictable, flying about practising her high notes, a sound that felt like shards of glass penetrating your eardrums. One thing was certain: she was very different from the other apprentices' nadims – all trusty beings that did their locksmiths' bidding without fuss. Celeste Clocks had a lemur that curled around her neck like a stole and slept peacefully when she wasn't working. Zeina Zaman had a fountain pen that could write messages in the air. They were useful, calm and reliable tools, while hers . . . Sometimes Aliya felt as though Simi wasn't a nadim at all, but something different altogether – a freakish entity with a mind of her own.

She suddenly became aware that the doorway they used for portal practice stood slightly ajar. Had Nigm not closed it properly? As she approached, Simi swooped down and alighted on her shoulder. Then, plunging forward, she pecked at the lock, probing it with her luminous beak. There was a pulse of light from under the door.

'What?' Aliya cried. 'What did you do?'

Aliya shot a glance over her shoulder through the window and into the corridor. Apprentices were not allowed to open portals without an authorized locksmith around, and whatever Simi did would count as *her* doing. Locksmiths and their nadims lived in symbiosis – like one soul, split into two bodies.

Aliya decided to have a quick peek. It had to be safe enough with the shield on.

For some moments, the opening showed nothing but darkness, an uncanny colour for an opening.

Aliya hesitated. She tried to grasp the nadim, who was fluttering by her head, to urge her to transform back into a key so they could lock the portal, but Simi resisted. Most of the time, all Aliya had to do was stroke her along her striped crest to get her to change. Instead of obeying, Simi squawked excitedly, her attention on the blackness of the portal. But they needed to close this rogue opening fast, before they were seen.

'Come *on*, Simi!' Aliya made another attempt to get the nadim to change.

Without Simi's compliance there was no way Aliya would be able to close the portal. She needed her key blade to turn the reverse way in the lock.

Something stirred in the darkness, glittering. Aliya thought it might be water at first, but then realized what she was seeing. It was scales – the scales of an enormous, black snake.

Aliya jerked backwards as the big head swung towards her. The snake's head shifted a little to the side, and now Aliya could see the sunken spot where its eye once had sat – the place Simi had come from.

The Darkling.

Aliya watched in horror as the snake probed the opening for a way to reach them. *Thank God the shield is still activated.* Hands shaking, she reached out and grabbed Simi firmly around her middle, catching her wings and pressing them down. What was *wrong* with her?

In front of her the Darkling swayed, its forked tongue shooting out and hitting the shield. Behind it, Aliya could make out a dim shop. It was the Shop of Second Chances, the locus of Dorian's magic.

'*Switch.*' Aliya gave Simi a sharp tap on the crest.

Simi finally complied, reshaping into a key in her hands. Aliya felt her palms light up as she inserted the key blade and turned it in reverse. The portal closed.

Aliya sank down on her haunches, her head swimming. Had she – or Simi – just opened a portal to the Shop of Second Chances? How was it possible? It *shouldn't* be possible.

Chapter 2
THE KEY WHISPERER

Aliya hurried down the bright corridor, her nadim safely tucked out of sight in her bag. She could feel Simi struggling in there. It would be a matter of time before she set the whole contents on fire. But Aliya had to keep her hidden until she could find out what was wrong with her. Because something had to be wrong. Why else would her nadim have thrown herself at the Darkling as if lovestruck? It had all happened in seconds. And worse: Simi had opened a portal to the Shop of Second Chances!

Aliya glanced down at her satchel. A thin pillar of smoke was rising from under the leather flap. *Opening a portal is always an act shared between nadim and locksmith*. She might unconsciously be responsible for openings to street-food joints, maybe even a Mongol raid, but this – this was different. Why would she want to access the Shop? No, this wouldn't do. She needed to consult an expert.

Deciding on a shortcut through the central lobby, she rounded the corner and pushed through a pair of double doors. The room inside was a flurry of winged mythical guards, hieracosphinxes, dancing in formation.

The mythicals would soon be performing at Qahira Square in celebration of the Great Race – the biggest event of the winter term, which was just three days away. The flying-carpet race went through a series of portals into different time periods, and everything in the Citadel had come to revolve around it. All the shops in the Fishawy Bazaar were selling Great Race merch, and the students at the time-travel academy could talk of nothing else. The race took place every two years, so this was the first time Aliya had a chance to be involved. Her own travel pod was aiming to qualify as Sweepers – back-up crews who followed the competing pods and closed the portals behind them. The try-outs were tonight.

In all this, Aliya felt at once excited and somewhat disappointed. It was the job of the locksmiths to set up the portals that made up the course, but because she was trying out, she couldn't take any part in its creation.

Now one of the hieracos stretched out a bulky paw, blocking her path.

'It wants you to give a message to your podmate Mustafa,' Celeste Clocks called from where she stood, directing the creatures' dance. Unlike the other types of sphinxes, who were very articulate, these winged beasts did not speak Human. Celeste had studied their grunts and caws and could understand them. Her mentor, Lahza Anwar, was in charge of the mythical guard – the Smithy's security.

'Tell him that they're looking for him,' Celeste interpreted. 'Something about an egg . . . a very special egg.'

Nodding, Aliya hurried on. She had no time right now for Mustafa and the hieracosphinxes' cryptic message. She pressed deeper into the Smithy, a place that seemed at once small and infinite. Since it only accommodated six senior locksmiths and their apprentices, along with a group of mythical guards and the grumps, the place often felt snug, just the right size. Yet at other times, the bright corridors seemed endless, with new vistas appearing behind great glass windows and marble staircases one had never noticed before, and that suddenly provided a much-needed passage or space. The truth was that the Smithy, just like the Infinitum itself, was mysterious and ever-expanding. Lit from within by the Sublimes — the mystical energy that animated the travel world — the workshop evolved and took on the shape its inhabitants needed, like a friendly, helpful spirit. Which is why Aliya, without quite knowing how, found herself exactly where she wanted to go.

A golden sign on the brass door read: KEY MAINTENANCE. This, she knew, was the domain of the key whisperer, a character she had heard about but never seen. Aliya pushed the heavy door open, then peered into the dim workshop where tall cabinets of differently sized boxes and parcels towered over a long, cluttered counter. Behind it, slumped on a stool, sat the oldest genie Aliya had ever seen. He was long and thin, with a big nose and elephant ears, and was concentrating intensely on peeling the brown wrapper off a sandwich. A radio was playing in a corner. As Aliya made her way down a short flight of stairs, the voice of the newscaster drifted towards her.

'During the night, tremors were felt in the Ancient Quarters, with a new crack appearing in the atmosphere above the Ptolemaian Quarter. An investigation into what could have caused the new disturbances is underway, says Inspector Peter Prickly of the Infinitum Security Services.'

The ancient genie was about to take the first toothless bite of his sandwich when he noticed Aliya and froze. An ample amount of marmalade slipped down his crooked fingers. With a sigh, he put the sandwich down and wiped his fingers on a napkin he fished out of the cuff of his shirt.

'What's the trouble?' He peered at her over half-moon glasses.

Aliya felt her face heating up. Apprentices

needed permission for everything they did at the Smithy, and she had none to be here. But she couldn't tell Nigm or anyone else what had just happened. It was one thing to be the bumbling novice, a sort of pet that everyone patted on the head and chuckled at. It was another to open a portal to the Shop of Second Chances. But she hadn't, had she? It hadn't been her.

'Hmm.' The genie looked from Aliya to her satchel and back again. 'Your bag is on fire.'

Aliya quickly unlatched the top of her satchel and tipped Simi out in a mess of smouldering papers. For a while, the countertop was thick with smoke. Aliya whipped frantically at it with a scorched notebook while the old genie coughed.

'It's my nadim,' she said when the smoke had cleared. 'She's not . . . right. I mean, she's not behaving well. I think there might be something wrong with her.'

'Did you ask her what's wrong?' the genie asked.

'Um, yeah . . . I tried, but—'

'Too much on your mind, eh?' The genie clicked his tongue.

Aliya bit her lower lip, praying the genie wouldn't ask any more questions – questions she wouldn't be able to answer. On the counter, Simi was ruffling her feathers, looking testy and bright. Even in her bird form she could heat up and glow, which explained the fire.

'Hmm.' The genie searched for something under the counter, then pulled out what looked like a doctor's stethoscope. Aliya had heard stories about the key whisperer. Halfway between a craftsman and a therapist, the old genie had his own way of maintaining the mysterious keys – ways that no one really knew how to describe.

Simi had begun attacking the marmalade sandwich, pecking at it with her curved beak. The key whisperer adjusted the stethoscope in his big ears, then leant over the counter and placed the listening bell smack in the middle of Aliya's forehead.

'But . . . it's not me,' she protested.

'Shh,' the genie said, listening intently. He moved the cool metal of the bell across Aliya's brow.

'Guilty,' he said finally, sitting back.

Aliya felt her throat tighten. *Guilty?* Did he mean

she was? For opening the portal just now? She looked over at the key whisperer, who was now examining Simi with his stethoscope. The old mythical sat back again, gathering up his instrument.

'She's homesick,' he said with a decisive nod. 'That's the trouble.'

Aliya stared at him.

'Home—' She frowned.

'—sick, yes.' The genie picked up his sandwich.

'But that doesn't make any sense,' Aliya said. 'Her home's with me.'

'Then you have not reached your final destination.' The key whisperer turned away from her on his swivel stool, his attention fully back on his lunch.

'But . . .' Aliya began again, but she had lost him. She heard a squelch of marmalade as he took a deep bite.

Aliya's confusion simmered into fear. Her final destination? The nadim had been part of the Darkling once. She had been the grain that made up its eye, that piece of Sublime spark that all travel keys needed to traverse time. But Aliya had freed her from the magic that had enslaved her, and Simi had stayed with her out of gratitude and become hers – or so it had seemed. But if Simi was striving to get back to the Darkling, if that was her destination . . . did she want to go back to Dorian, to *magic*?

She carefully lifted the nadim on to her shoulder, feeling the weight of the luminous bird's body. She felt strangely heavy. Could there still be some magic left in Simi? Thanking the key whisperer, she headed back out into the maze of corridors.

Aliya stopped outside the carpet nursery, where the other locksmith apprentices were gathered around workbenches, helping Janus Quartz, one of the locksmith professors, to vitalize race carpets in preparation for the Great Race. The air was alive with Persians and Shirazis, zooming this way and that, luminous with the energy the locksmith had charged them with. Aliya watched as a dark-blue carpet got frisky, knocking one of the apprentices off his feet, then carrying him off in a flurry of tassels and carpet dust.

'*There* you are!'

Aliya turned to find Arsinoe, an apprentice from the Ptolemaic age, scowling down at her. Despite the chaos in the nursery, she looked poised and stylish. Looking at her, you would never have guessed she'd suffered through a terrible ordeal on board the *Silver Express* chrono-train last summer, when Dorian Darke had trapped her soul in a mirror and worn her body like a suit. That Aliya had been instrumental in saving her life hadn't warmed Arsinoe to her. Aliya sometimes felt that quite the opposite was true, as if the senior resented being in her debt.

'Nigm asked me to find you,' Arsinoe said now. 'To make sure you got home all right. I really hadn't expected to have to scour the whole Smithy looking for you.'

Aliya gave Simi a quick glance.

'Um . . . sorry,' she said. 'Just went for a walk.'

Arsinoe arched an eyebrow. No one went for random 'walks' inside the Smithy. Many corridors and rooms were off limits because they housed secret projects. Just two weeks ago, Professor Nigm had moved their apprentice sessions out of his workshop because of some project he wouldn't tell her about. Secrecy was the norm at the Smithy. It could be annoying at times, being kept out of so many things. And Aliya, as the newest apprentice, knew least of all what was going on.

'Well, I'm to escort you out, just as soon as you've cleared up in there.' Arsinoe pointed at a snack table at the end of the carpet nursery, where the locksmiths had caught the last of the wild carpets and were packing up.

'Wait, why do I have to clean up *again*?' Aliya protested. 'I didn't even get any of the snacks.'

'Pecking order, sorry.' Arsinoe did not sound even a bit apologetic. Aliya wondered if it actually was an order or just something the senior had made up. 'You should be thankful you're not on hieracosphinx duty.'

Aliya sighed.

'OK, *fine*.' Anything was better than cleaning up the poos that the hulking mythical guards left lying in the corridors. Thankfully, they mostly used the scoop-and-wipe robots for that.

Inside the workshop, Professor Quartz was tucking

into a piece of red eish saray, a syrupy bread pudding spread with a thick layer of cream.

'Oh, Anisa,' he called out when he saw Aliya approaching with the clean-up cart. 'Please remove this death trap.' He pointed at the snack table with its generous spread of oriental sweets. 'We'll have sugar syrup for blood if Cook doesn't stop sending this every coffee break!'

'My name is Aliya,' Aliya muttered, unhooking a broom and padding over to the spread of used mugs, plates and half-full glasses.

A voice called from the door: 'Are you done, Professor? We're all here and ready to go.' It was Omar again. 'Bye, Aliya,' he added with a smirk. 'Enjoy the clean-up!'

Aliya stabbed the floor with the broom. While she was stuck clearing up their mess, the rest of the apprentices were off to assist their mentors in the creation of the racecourse. Two years previously, they had opened portals from the Byzantine era to the Ottoman, with a jump to 1950s Cairo. The older apprentices still talked about the fun they'd had, and all the magnificent dinners Professor Quartz had invited them to in the different times.

Once alone, Aliya gave Simi a mini chocolate croissant to peck. Nadims didn't really eat, but Simi enjoyed discovering new textures. Aliya found some discarded newspapers on the table, and was about to wrap up some eish saray to take back to the hostel when a few headlines caught her attention:

DIVIDED LOYALTIES?
EX-COLLEAGUES OF DORIAN DARKE
STILL IN PROMINENT SMITHY ROLES

TICKER DEFENDS LOCKSMITHS,
BUT SUGGESTS COUNCIL SHOULD HAVE
GREATER ACCESS TO SMITHY

MYTHICALS AMONG US: COULD THEIR
POWERS BE KEEPING TEARS OPEN?

It wasn't news to Aliya that many human travellers were suspicious of the mythicals. Ever since she'd arrived at the Citadel, there had been whispering about them, about the ghouls and the genies, the sphinxes and silas – accusing them of never really giving up the habit of using magic, which was banned in the travel world. But these headlines were suggesting that the *locksmiths* were bad, and to refer to them as 'ex-colleagues of Dorian Darke' was surely going too far? As far as she knew, the locksmiths were revered as the ones closest to the Sublimes. It was they who channelled their power and made it useful to the travel community. Aliya scanned the names of the papers: *The Evening Chronometer*, *The Traveller's Digest* and *You Heard It Here First!*

Tabloid press. She ripped out the worst pages and used them to wrap up her sweets. Nothing to take seriously, she decided.

She had just resumed sweeping when it began. A hum, deep and resonant, rang through the air. It enfolded her like a fog, coming from the walls, the ceiling, the ground. It was a sound at once bewildering and familiar – the voice of the Sublimes. A memory stirred within her. By now it had become so familiar that she relished it whenever it resurfaced. There she was, a child still, in her mother's locksmith workshop, on the back of a golden dragon with a mane like fire, soaring through the large room, touching the high ceiling, then dipping again. Her mother, who stood by a workbench, looked up briefly and smiled, her slender hands busily manoeuvring silvery instruments.

The voice of the Sublimes pulled at her like a current, and Aliya followed it towards the source of the sound. She had reached the silver door that marked the entrance to the deep cave where the Sublimes resided, when another sound cut through the air – a scream. It was coming from inside the cave.

Aliya was about to push the heavy door open when Arsinoe appeared, forcing her back into the corridor. She was dishevelled and wild-eyed, but the strangest thing about her was her hands. All locksmiths were alike in that their palms lit up with Sublime energy when they worked. But Arsinoe's hands were blackened, as if she had dipped them in soot. A moment later, she had pulled on a pair of leather gloves.

'What are you doing here?' Arsinoe's eyes were hard. 'Were you *spying* on me?'

The Sublimes' low hum still hung in the air around them.

'No, I wasn't, I swear. I just heard something—'

'I stubbed my toe when I was closing up in there.'

Arsinoe started down the corridor, pulling Aliya with her. An odd burnt smell hung around them as they marched towards the lobby where the exit portal was. What had the senior been up to in the Sublimes' cave?

Arsinoe had spent the beginning of the term at the sanatorium with her chameleon nadim, Proteus, to recover from Dorian disembodying her on the *Silver Express*. All the magician's victims had spent time there, but the senior had been there the longest. The attack had severed her connection to her nadim, a trauma that had turned him black and made Arsinoe temporarily lose her locksmith powers. At the Smithy, they had all been waiting for the pair to recover, but progress was slow. There were even whispers that she'd never be a proper locksmith again. Arsinoe, who had always been popular, had received a lot of support from her peers. Still, she'd been strangely quiet since she got back, and often seemed to be in a fretful mood, able to perform only the most basic locksmith tasks.

When they had reached the lobby, the senior gestured towards the exit portal.

'Go ahead, then. Let's see what you can do.'

Aliya stared at her.

'You want me to open it?'

Aliya's growing portal-blunder reputation meant the other locksmiths never let her open the exit portal.

'Yes,' Arsinoe huffed impatiently. 'I stayed behind for you, didn't I? To teach you something. So go ahead, practise!'

Aliya turned to the portal. Something about this situation did not add up. Why was Arsinoe volunteering to stay behind instead of participating in preparing the racecourse – the most exciting locksmith event of the season? Arsinoe didn't even like her.

Taking a deep breath, Aliya stroked Simi along her striped crest, then watched as she transformed into a key that fitted perfectly in the lock before her. *Matron Olfat's Scholastic Hostel*, Aliya thought. There was a satisfying *click* as the nadim turned in the lock and a pulse of light appeared under the door.

Shoving her aside, Arsinoe opened it. Aliya exhaled in relief as the familiar facade of her student hostel loomed into sight. It had worked for once. They stepped through the watery surface of the portal, opaque if seen from the outside, and just big enough to let them through. No one on the outside would be able to move in the other way, or even peek into the Smithy.

'A quick question!' someone called as Aliya closed the portal behind them. As she began crossing the square, a pixie reporter whom she recognized from the local Citadel channel stuck a microphone under her nose. The pixie, along with her broadcasting equipment, was floating a metre above ground to reach eye level with Aliya.

'What do you – the apprentice of the notorious Professor Nigm – say to the rumours circulating about him and the other locksmiths?' The small reporter floated closer, her microphone bobbing just under Aliya's nose.

'Notorious?' Aliya frowned. She wasn't even sure

what it meant. This was the second time today that she'd encountered strange talk about the locksmiths.

'Ah, yes.' The pixie's eyes narrowed conspiratorially. 'All the secrets you lot have, like that mysterious workshop that no outsider ever gets to visit. It's no wonder that people begin to get suspicious . . .' She gestured at where the portal had just vanished, again becoming the door to the hostel sphinxes' loo. Aliya usually exited the Smithy through there. Had the reporter found out and been waiting for her?

Arsinoe intervened, leading Aliya towards Matron Olfat's hostel. Behind them the pixie reporter called: 'The truth's bound to come out some time! You know what I'm talking about!'

'What *is* she talking about?' Aliya asked Arsinoe as they reached the entrance of the hostel, Aliya's home in the time-travel world.

'Oh, you know what the Citadel press is like, always stirring up trouble . . . although, she's right, isn't she? Haven't you ever wondered why there are so many locked doors in the Smithy, so many secret projects?'

'Just because they're secret doesn't mean something fishy is going on.'

Arsinoe shrugged. Aliya looked at her in bewilderment. How could she speak like this when they were both locksmiths? At least in the making.

'Dorian Darke was a locksmith,' Arsinoe continued. 'They're saying his closeness to so much Sublime power is what corrupted him.'

'So? That doesn't mean anything.'

'Doesn't it?' Arsinoe smiled. It was the first smile Aliya had seen from her for a long time. 'Maybe we've got a tendency, more than others, to step over boundaries we shouldn't?'

With that, she turned and walked off across the square without a backwards glance. Her words tugged at Aliya. Just hours before, she had opened the portal to the Shop and seen the Darkling's black scales slide past her in the darkness. She had felt a pull then, in her heart, as if she had recognized something.

Pushing the thought away, she lingered by the entrance, cold and miserable, watching the pixie reporter, who had begun quarrelling with the sphinxes who guarded the hostel, tauntingly floating over their shaggy heads. The sphinxes, who were part-cat, were swiping excitedly at the stray cables that hung down from her recording equipment.

Aliya wasn't very familiar with the journalistic practices of the travel world, but she often read the papers at breakfast for their strange titbits of news. The genie reporters, who could slip through keyholes and turn invisible at will, were like paparazzi on another level. Last month, they had reported that Matron Olfat, who ran Aliya's student hostel, used a piranha fishtank to give herself a pedicure, and that Inspector Prickly, who was head of Infinitum Security, had been chased around the Victorian Quarter by one of his own security robots.

Those reports, although cheeky, had always been in good humour, but this was different. They had never insinuated foul play before. And to suspect the locksmiths of . . . what, exactly? There were also the new tremors in the time-travel world that Aliya had heard about on the key whisperer's radio. How did they fit into things? Something strange was brewing, an invisible undercurrent that could be felt but not yet seen.

Chapter 3
THE RACE PODS

Aliya entered the hostel to find ghoul maids flying around on carpets, brandishing cleaning tools. In the courtyard stood the hostel matron, Olfat, directing the dusting of her ancestral portraits. It was Great-Cousin Morbidus's turn to be cleaned. Aliya winced, wishing they hadn't bothered, as Morbidus appeared from behind the thick coat of dust and grime. The bucktoothed, beady-eyed, unibrowed face that peered down at her was a slightly scarier version of the ghoul matron's, with an added expression that seemed to say: *Will you be my dinner?*

In the few hours she had been away at the Smithy, the hostel had undergone quite a transformation. The thick dust had been blown out of the corners and the gargoyles in the central fountain had been dressed in black outfits with ruffled collars. Bunting, made of what Aliya suspected were dried bats, hung in ominous loops across the balconies of different floors.

Aliya gazed up at the glossy poster of the hostel's own racing pod, affectionately known as 'The Ghoulies'. At the centre stood Salman Bashiri, the pod's navigator – a bulky senior with a wide smile and a braided beard. Salman was part-troll, which explained his excessive hair growth and thunderous laughter.

'Over here, dearie!' A bright voice snapped Aliya out of her thoughts. Mrs Dickens, the hostel cook, stood in the doorway to the kitchen, holding a basket of golden-brown scones. Behind her the big kitchen spread out, full of bubbling pots, sizzling pans and stacks of dog-eared cookbooks. In contrast to the rest of the ghoul hostel, Mrs Dickens's domain was a bright place full of colour, from the sunflower-printed curtains to the large vase of tulips on the long wooden table where the staff ate.

'Will you be a dear and bring these with you to

the upper terrace?' Mrs Dickens put the basket into Aliya's arms and patted her on the cheek. 'You'll be having lunch there today. Your friends are already up there watching the race pods practise. Oh, I love when the Great Race comes around. It's all so exciting and so stimulating for the appetite! Go on now, dear. You'd better hurry.'

'I'll go straight up.' Aliya inhaled the mouth-watering aroma of the scones. The smell was enough to make the thoughts of her gloomy morning evaporate. Suddenly all she could think about was lunch – Mrs Dickens's lunch.

Aliya stepped out on to the terrace that had been prepared for the students. An array of mismatched furniture, borrowed from the various grades' common rooms, was dotted around. The November air was crisp, with enough winter sun to make eating outdoors pleasant. They were halfway through the school year already, but this was the first time they had got to eat outside. From this roof, the view of the city seemed never-ending. On the horizon, Aliya could discern the pyramids of the Ancient

Quarter, their gold tops catching the sun. To the right was 'Little Ben', the Victorian Quarter's version of the London clock tower. The rest of the city stretched out in all its patchwork glory, with the oldest quarters furthest away and the areas getting more modern as you moved towards where she stood. The Khedivial Quarter, where the hostel lay, was among the modern areas, although the concepts of old and new were fluid and ever-changing in the travel world. Snaking through the city, its water glittering in the sun, was the great Salsabil River – the town's jugular vein.

'*About time!*' Aliya's classmate, Victoria Prickly, snatched the basket of scones out of her hands and deposited it on the cart of a passing ghoul maid. 'I don't know how you could disappear for hours when we've got a try-out to plan!'

That evening Aliya and her pod were trying out for a spot as Sweepers to the Ghoulies, closing portals in the seniors' wake and reporting any incidents to Race HQ back in the Citadel.

There was only one other pod from their hostel competing to sweep for the Ghoulies – some third-graders Victoria had nicknamed 'The Nepos' because she thought of them as 'nepo babies'– kids who had an advantage because of being related to an older, successful traveller. That was because their navigator, Francesca Flux, was first cousins with the Ghoulies' chronologer, Charles.

Since term began, Victoria had set her heart on their pod getting to be Sweepers. Trying out was a great way of getting ahead. It showed gumption – something the Council appreciated. But it was also risky. If a pod didn't cooperate well on such a public stage, the Council might decide to disband them. They could be branded as 'troublesome' or 'difficult to work with', the worst possible qualities in time-travellers, whose missions required complete loyalty and effortless teamwork. Disbanded members usually ended up working in administration or as 'duds' who minded portals in the earthly sphere, or in other jobs. But none of them involved 'real' missions to other times.

'I didn't disappear,' Aliya said as Victoria pulled her past a loaded food cart. 'I have apprentice duties, you know.'

Around them, the terrace was full of students from different years, sitting in clusters, eating. Aliya's mouth watered at the sight of the scrumptious displays on the tables. Mrs Dickens's food was one of the few things students from the other hostels envied about Matron Olfat's.

'The Nepos think they've got the trial in the bag.' Victoria glared at a table a little way off, where Francesca and her friends sat sharing a large feteer with honey and cream. The crispy pancakes were one of Mrs Dickens's specialities, with layer upon layer of flaky crust that became deliciously gooey when smothered in honey and eshta – the thick cream made of water-buffalo milk.

'They've been sucking up to the Ghoulies.' Victoria gestured up at one of the suspended banners. 'Waiting on them hand and foot, giving them gifts . . . Last night they gave Salman a whole box of raw fish, which he loved, of course, since he's a troll . . . Ah, damnation! Why didn't *we* think of that? We could've done what they did and grovelled. Come to think of it, that's your new mission. Learn to grovel!' She set off towards the Nepos' table.

Scanning the terrace for the ambulant food cart, Aliya caught sight of her classmate Mustafa by the balustrade, gazing up at the sky. As always, he was the most neatly turned out of their pod, in his ironed shirt and the second year's blue tarboosh, the round felt hat with a black tassel that all the male students wore (the girls had matching berets). Mustafa actually woke up in time to iron his clothes in the morning. That made a contrast to his roommate, Fuad, whose idea of ironing was to leave his shirts on Matron's armchair so that they would flatten when the bulky ghoul sat on them. He also washed his socks by wearing them in the shower. As second-graders, they were expected to do their own laundry.

Aliya glanced down at her uniform. After finally qualifying as a real time-travel student, she had been allowed to exchange her temporary velvet training suit to dress like her classmates. It was a delicious feeling to blend in, even though her uniform looked like it had been chewed on by a rabid sphinx (she really should ask Mustafa to teach her the art of ironing). Even so, the uniform made it a fact: she wasn't the odd one out any more, at least not here with her peers. What happened in the Smithy with the locksmith apprentices was another story.

'Hey,' Aliya said when she reached Mustafa. 'Some hieracosphinxes are looking for you.'

Mustafa turned to her, eyes wide. He scanned the terrace in panic.

'Where are they?'

'Not here, at the Smithy,' Aliya said. 'What's going on? They said it had something to do with an egg?'

'Oh, yes, that.' Mustafa pulled nervously at his tie. 'I've been given a special job over at the Refuge, looking after an unhatched egg. I hardly slept last night, or any other night for weeks. There've been some disappearances over there. Mythicals vanishing. It's really strange.'

Aliya nodded. Mustafa did look a bit green. And come to think of it, she had hardly seen her podmate these past few weeks. He was always working over at the Refuge – the place where new mythicals were kept until they were deemed safe enough to join the travelling community. As an apprentice at the Care of Mythical Creatures Department, he dealt with dangerous mythicals on a daily basis and, apparently, their unhatched eggs.

'I'm not sure what's worse,' he said. 'Not sleeping or being scared all the time. Last week, the hieracos sent me worms in an envelope. *Worms*. Some were crushed, even. The other apprentices said it was meant as a nice gesture, you know, sending me a snack, but I'm not sure. Do you think it means they'll crush me like a worm if something happens to their egg?'

Aliya, who didn't speak Hieracosphinx, shrugged.

'Are you sure one didn't follow you?' Mustafa asked again.

But Aliya had caught sight of something else that made her forget all about hieracos. Grabbing him by the arm, she pointed at the sky. There was a low swooshing sound that gradually grew in volume. Around her the assembled students stopped eating. *This* was why they had come up here this afternoon. Many dropped their cutlery and rushed over to the balustrade for a better view, staring up at the early afternoon sky, which suddenly came alive as one, then two, then three flying carpets soared overhead at breakneck speed, looking as though they were about to crash into the hostel roof. It was the competing pods: the Ghoulies from Matron Olfat's hostel, the Janissaries from Mehmet Nazim's in the Ottoman Quarter, and the Philosophers from Madame Hippolyta's in the Ptolemaic Quarter.

Just as Aliya felt sure the race pods were going to be smashed to pulp, the speed-blurred rider on the foremost carpet stretched out a hand. There was a blast of light and the wide skylight in the tiled roof turned into a portal. In seconds, the three pods and their carpets were swallowed by the opening, making the hostel look like it had grown a lopsided mouth.

The crowd of students caught their breath before erupting in a wild cheer.

'Did you see how fast he opened that portal?' Mustafa shouted, pointing. 'And they're not even locksmiths!'

Aliya nodded approvingly, but not without a twinge of sadness. Opening portals was supposed to be her forte as a locksmith, but even these travellers were far ahead of her in skill. Then again, they *were* seniors.

An amused cheer went through the crowd as another, slower carpet came into view. On board sat a lady Aliya recognized. It was Miss Prim, the stern minder who had guided her through her assessments during her first term. With her tight ballerina bun and stiff posture, the minder looked as disapproving as ever. Ignoring the cheers from below, Miss Prim steered her carpet towards the open portal. With a firm reverse turn of her key, she closed it.

The students responded with another cheer, which the minder ignored. She was about to retreat the way she had come when the skylight burst open once more. Shooting out in quick succession came the senior pods, one after the other. So sudden was their reappearance, and so close to the minder, that they knocked her off her carpet. After a half-somersault backwards, Miss Prim was left clinging to its tail end.

The Ghoulies quickly circled back and helped the enraged minder back aboard, and then closed the portal they had opened. Below, Aliya and the rest of the students watched in fascination. The speed of the senior pods, their quickness in portal opening – it was a heady mixture.

The seniors took off again, and Aliya remembered how ravenous she was. She'd been on the terrace for about fifteen minutes already and hadn't eaten a single bite of food.

Aliya found her best friend and roommate Karima at a table fiddling with a large spray can. It smelt terrible, and Aliya's stomach growled in protest. Karima was a medic in training and was always developing some new recipe based on menacin – the ghoulish art of healing. Aliya had learnt to live with the putrid smells, but it would've been nice to avoid them at mealtimes.

'What *is* that?' she asked, pinching her nose closed.

'Fermented nereid spit.' Karima looked up with a quick smile. 'Great for reviving someone who has passed out, especially out of fear. Mustafa asked for it. He's afraid he'll lose his position at the Refuge if he keeps fainting every time a Roc bird caws at him.'

They giggled. The girls had been roommates since Aliya's first day in the travel world. That had only been a little more than a year ago, but they had already been through enough adventures to last them a lifetime. Aliya had spent a blissful end of summer vacation with Karima and her twin brother Fuad, soaking up the Mediterranean sun at their chalet in Alexandria. Lounging in the sand, nibbling mangoes and freska, the wafer sweets sold by ambulant sellers – it had been bliss. In the evenings, they had roller-skated along the curved seafront or gone to the cinema. The twins came from the 1930s, and Aliya had relished the feeling of being in a different time which was at once so familiar and so different from her own Egypt. The only downside had been her necessary, and frequent, visits to the chronobaric chamber, hidden away in a fellow traveller's flat, where she'd had to spend a few hours every three days to prevent her body from feeling the ill effects of being in a time other than her own. Still, it had been a glorious end to the summer, especially after the horrific events she'd lived through on board the *Silver Express*.

But as the term had progressed her friends had grown increasingly busy, and she often found herself alone, at breakfast, at dinner, and in the pod's common room during the long winter evenings.

Apart from the times they had spent preparing for tonight's try-outs, she had hardly seen them. This was the first time she and Karima had sat down at a table together in for ever. Aliya nodded over Karima's shoulder at Victoria, who was hovering by the Nepos' table, peeking over their shoulders, as if she suspected that the feteer they were eating contained secret plans.

'So, Victoria's keeping a healthy perspective on things? She suggested I grovel. That's new.'

Karima nodded. 'She's gone absolutely ballistic. She's convinced the Nepos have an advantage over us . . . which they might. They're only one year older, yes, but that means they had a practice run at the try-outs two years ago, when they were first-graders.'

'But we went over our strategy *four* times last night,' Aliya said. 'And once this morning, before I went off to the Smithy. I think I did it in my sleep.'

Victoria had appeared in the girls' room that morning and forced them to repeat the strategy for tonight's try-outs. She had even made the bedpost guardians join in. The old-lady faces that were carved into the posts of Karima's and Aliya's beds were meant to protect them when they slept. But now, since Victoria had begun harassing them in their room at all hours, the guardians (who tended to repeat things) had begun shouting commands at random – *Stake out the area! Look for portals! Report back! Regroup!*

A pair of ghoul maids pushing a food cart stalked past and Aliya gave them a desperate wave.

'Wot'll it be, love?' said the biggest of the ghouls, gesturing at his assortment of pies which, up close, were a mess of disgusting things. 'Fancy a slice of booger bonanza? 'Ow about this snotty surprise?'

'No – no, thanks.' Aliya tried to turn away, but the second ghoul insisted.

'Ah, come on, love.' She pushed a plate of what looked like small, crusty half-moons at Aliya. ''Ave some nail clippings. They're toasted!'

'Ah, come off it!' Karima snapped at the big ghoul. 'You promised Ma you wouldn't.'

The wonky-teethed maids blurred. A moment later, Aliya's classmates Fuad and Aion appeared, dressed from head to toe in sleek, silvery suits. Aliya could have kicked herself. *Of course.* Fuad, who was an apprentice at the Stealth Department, had recently joined forces with Aion, a travel-inventions specialist in training, to invent things they claimed could 'benefit their pod'. The outcomes were equal parts brilliant and annoying, especially since Aliya and the rest of her pod were the constant guinea pigs.

'Got ya!' Fuad cried with glee. He turned to Aion, who was peeling off a thin, silvery mask. 'We're brilliant, Aion. We're actually brilliant.'

'*She* is,' Karima grumbled to her brother. 'You're just a lousy prankster.'

'Not the smartsuits again,' Aliya groaned.

'*Yes*, the smartsuits!' Fuad beamed. 'They're the best thing since smores and remote controls.'

A little later, Aliya finally got something good to eat when the whole pod assembled around one of Mrs Dickens's enormous feteers.

'We've still got to decide who'll be closing the portals tonight,' Victoria said, fingers dripping with honey. 'My feeling is that I should take care of it.'

'And why's that?' Aliya asked. 'We've all got our keys now.'

As second-graders, the pod had received their travel keys. These were made in the Smithy, in the Sublime furnace, where the mysterious energy source shaped the key blade to suit each traveller's character. Fuad's was, unsurprisingly, in the shape of a wily mongoose, while Karima's was a trusty, excitable golden retriever. Mustafa's key was a beautiful hare, while Aion had a desert mouse. The pod had had a good laugh when Victoria showed them her key – a golden rhinoceros. Thick-skinned, blunt, with no concept of fear, the animal did suit her, Aliya thought. Still, Victoria seemed happy with the outcome.

'You're a navigator,' Mustafa told Victoria in his mild manner. 'Is there any reason why you would be best suited to closing portals?'

For the last two weeks, the pod had been training for the Sweeper try-outs at night in the quiet park next to the hostel, working on their flying-carpet skills and pretending to close a portal made out of an old doorway they had propped up between two trees. As Sweepers, that would be one of their main tasks.

As for the try-outs, none of them knew exactly

what they entailed, only that their main aim was to test a pod's ability to cooperate, to think on its feet, and to problem-solve.

Victoria was an excellent navigator, but often got so caught up in her instruments that she forgot to steer the carpet. Only last week, she had got entangled in the branches of one of the park's jacaranda trees.

'I think it should be Aliya,' Karima said. 'She's a locksmith, isn't she? That's their thing, to deal with portals.'

Victoria harrumphed.

'The business of locksmiths is to *create* portals. That doesn't make them any better at opening or closing them.'

It was something that Victoria often pointed out: locksmiths were *no* better than any other form of traveller, even though that was often the way they were talked about – as mysterious, elevated and special. Aliya glanced at Simi, who was attacking a piece of feteer with her curved beak. Her nadim certainly did not make a very convincing argument for Aliya being the best choice for key handler.

'I don't mind steering the carpet.' Aliya shrugged. 'That's enough for me.'

'Well, good,' Victoria said. 'And anyway, it might be better for you to take a back seat at this point, considering all the talk that's going around.'

'What talk?' Aliya looked around at her friends. 'You mean about the locksmiths? You don't mean you care about what those tabloid papers are writing?'

Aliya, who had expected an instant dismissal of the crazy rumours, was stunned when the others exchanged glances.

'Well, some of the things they write *are* kind of true,' Fuad said, with an awkward smile. 'The secrecy . . . I mean, why isn't anyone ever allowed into the Smithy?'

'They think they're superior to everyone else,' Victoria said with a decisive nod. 'Just look at Arsinoe. I heard her bragging to one of the seniors in my department about the secret projects your lot are up to. It was almost as if she *wanted* us to suspect them.'

Aliya thought of what Arsinoe had told her about the locksmiths earlier that day – that they had a 'tendency' to be drawn to evil. Sure, people whispered about the locksmiths being secretive and superior, but always, she had thought, with a sense of awe, not like this – not with suspicion.

'There've been quite a few articles recently – it means everyone's talking about the locksmiths,' Mustafa explained to Aliya. 'But I'm sure it'll blow over.'

'My parents told me the locksmiths are elitist or something,' Aion mumbled.

'Didn't you say your mentor is up to some secret project in his workshop?' Fuad grinned at her. Aliya was unsure if he really suspected Professor Nigm of anything, or was just trying to rile her, something she wouldn't put past him.

'OK, that's enough.' Karima glanced at Aliya. 'They're just rumours after all.'

'Dorian Darke *was* a locksmith,' Victoria insisted. 'That's not a rumour. That's a fact.'

'What are you saying, exactly?' Aliya felt her anger begin to build. How dare they accuse her and her mentor of being elitist, of being up to no good, of hiding away doing shady projects? She felt Karima's hand on her arm, but ignored it. 'If the locksmiths are all of those things, then I guess that includes me too? Am I *elitist*?' She glared at Victoria. She should talk. If anyone was Miss High-and-Mighty, it was her. 'Am I *dangerous*?'

'Oh, come on,' Fuad said. 'We're just messing with you.'

'I obviously wasn't talking about you,' Victoria said. 'You're not even a proper locksmith yet.'

'Oh, well, that's all right, then,' Aliya snapped. 'Silly me!'

'Some of the articles *are* pretty convincing, though,' Karima said, her hand still on Aliya's arm. 'And I admit to getting a bit confused about the locksmiths when I read them, but knowing you . . . and Professor Nigm . . . it makes no sense.'

'No, it doesn't.' Mustafa looked troubled.

Aliya frowned.

'Well, I'm so relieved you don't think I'm a criminal.'

'Enough about that.' Victoria put down her teacup. 'Back to planning. Aliya will be in charge of the carpet. Mustafa and I will work together to localize the portal. Fuad and Aion will keep us hidden, and Karima . . . I guess we'll need refreshments afterwards. Oh, and I'll be in charge of closing the portal.'

'No, Karima should do it,' cut in Aliya, who felt an urgent need to contradict Victoria. 'Close the portal, I mean. I don't see why you get two tasks and she none.'

Victoria rolled her eyes. Karima, who was a medic in training, would normally be in charge of healing or feeding the pod members, but tonight neither would be required, unless they had some sort of accident. And even then, there would probably be medical staff on standby at the try-outs.

'Mum and Dad will be attending tonight,' Karima said with a grateful smile at Aliya. 'After what happened on the *Silver Express* last summer, Mum's got all worked up again about me being here. It would be good to show them what we can do.'

'What's new?' Victoria said. 'Papa doesn't say anything, but I know he still thinks I would be better off back home with my governess, learning to pickle things and embroider.' Victoria's father was

Inspector Peter Prickly, head of Infinitum Security.

The fact that Dorian Darke had nearly done away with them aboard the *Silver Express* had not exactly helped convince him or anyone else's parents or families that the travel world was the best place for them to be. That Dorian Darke had been on the train was not the official story, of course, but several parents had still withdrawn their children from their hostels and brought them home, fearful that the unconfirmed rumours were true.

'My mum says the Infinitum's changed for the worse,' Aion said. 'That it's not safe any more, like it was when they were students. They even tried to make me attend holographically this year.' Aion and the rest of the Verge family lived in the 2090s.

'We're going to stick to the basics,' Victoria said, standing up to leave. 'That means no showing off with fancy, useless tech –' she stared at Fuad and Aion – 'or helping *anyone other than our pod members*.' Here she looked at Mustafa and Karima who, during the practice in the park, had helped two squirrels (a broken leg, a raided nut stash). 'And for God's sake, control your *weird bird*!' The last comment was aimed at Aliya and Simi who, at that very moment, was dipping her beak in the honey jug.

Aliya was about to protest, to come to Simi's defence, but the thought of the nadim's behaviour that morning made her hesitate.

As the meal drew to an end, Aliya, who still felt sore about the pod's suspicions about the locksmiths, slipped away to be alone. As she climbed the winding staircase towards the attic where her grandfather stayed, her anger at the rumours gave way to worry. What if the others had known about what had happened that morning, when she had accidentally opened that portal to the Shop? What would they think of her then?

Chapter 4
A MAKESHIFT BRIGADE

Aliya stopped at the top of the stairs to catch her breath. The door to her grandfather's rooms was closed and the electric elevator chair that Matron had installed for him was not in its usual parked position at the top of the banister. Her heart sank. She had hoped he'd be in. Right now, she'd give anything just to sit with him and feel the world, which had begun to fragment into new uncertainties, come together again. The way this worked was wordless. Geddo wasn't much of a talker, more of a presence – a soothing, stable one. Maybe that was why she liked Professor Nigm, who talked with smoke, not words. It felt familiar. Her and Geddo's comforting togetherness had been made through routines – habits that had carried over from their Cairo lives.

One such habit was late-night sausages and eggs in front of the TV. They usually watched old black and white Egyptian movies, and Geddo always fell asleep before the end. Sometimes Aliya did too, and she'd wake up thinking they were back in their flat in Cairo, in a time before she knew anything about the travel world. Another routine was to play backgammon on the balcony while listening to old Arabic songs. When Geddo joined in, crooning the lyrics in his gravelly voice, it was as if his heart opened, spilling out his innermost thoughts . . . of love and loss and sorrow. There was always something heavy about Geddo; perhaps that was the thing that made him silent.

Fishing out her own key, Aliya unlocked the door and made her way through to the dark living room, where Geddo's large armchair stood in front of the fireplace. She sank down on her own chair next to it and stared into the unlit grate. Just like her podmates, Geddo had been busy lately, disappearing for hours on end. Aliya hadn't pressed him to tell her what it was he got up to. She hoped he was being treated for the stab wound Dorian had inflicted on him over a year ago – it still hadn't healed properly, and Matron Olfat's menacin expertise was one of the main reasons he was living at the student hostel. Matron's skill hadn't stopped Aliya and Karima trying to develop their own menacin cure for Geddo, just in case. At least they had been, before Karima had got too busy with other things.

'Oi, you . . . girl with the weird bird.' The voice made Aliya jerk in shock. Turning, she found one of the ghoul maids. 'Your grandfather has a message for you.'

The ghoul maids had a habit of appearing soundlessly, and for a moment Aliya wondered if she had passed through the wall. Then she saw that she had left the front door ajar.

'Which is?' Aliya said when the maid said nothing more, but merely smiled at her in an unsettling way. Like most ghoul maids Aliya knew, this one had that eerie habit of leaving long pauses in conversation, during which you weren't sure what they were going to do next.

'You need to come with me,' the maid said, turning on her heel and heading for the door. Aliya got up and followed.

The maid led her through the long, dim corridors of the upmost floor until they reached an out-of-the-way spiral staircase she'd never noticed before. This didn't surprise her. The hostel was full of secret passages and stairways one did best to avoid. Many stories told of students who had fallen through portals and ended up in other times. The more sinister tales described how students had been eaten by cupboard-dwelling beasts, but Aliya wasn't sure those were true. Scaring the students witless was one of the ghoul maids' favourite pastimes. Still, she did not venture anywhere unfamiliar in the hostel if she could help it.

'Just stand there,' the ghoul maid told Aliya as they stepped on to the spiral staircase. 'And hold on to the railing.'

Aliya took a firm grip as the staircase began turning downwards, like a drill. Down and down they went, as if through a rabbit hole. On all sides, Aliya could see nothing but stone walls. It got darker, until all she could see was the glinting of the maid's front teeth as she grinned. They were really in the bowels of the hostel now, drilling yet deeper.

When Aliya was close to panicking for real, the stairs stopped with a jerk.

The ghoul, who was clearly enjoying Aliya's unease, waved for her to follow. A doorway appeared in the gloom.

'What is this place?' Aliya stumbled off the staircase.

'A secret lair, of course.'

The moment Aliya stepped through the door, something big flew past her, grazing her cheek – *a pygmy goblin*. Aliya ducked as another one came flying: wrinkled, bright pink and about the size of a tennis ball. It was chuckling maniacally. This one, she realized, was grasping a bunch of hair.

'Come back here!'

A thin man in a lime-green suit shot past in pursuit. His white hair hung to his shoulders, but the top of his head was bald. This, Aliya knew, was Jax Jaxson, the bomb-defusing expert from the Infinitum SWAT team Geddo had once led – the Brigade.

'Abort! Abort!' shouted Geddo, who sat slumped in his wheelchair in a corner of the large, cavernous room, next to his sister Gigi and the hostel matron. So, was this what Geddo had been up to? Not getting treatment during all those evenings he'd left her alone, but instead reuniting his old SWAT team?

Geddo was pointing at a seemingly ordinary box, which stood open at the centre of the floor.

'It's a Pandora Box,' said a voice next to Aliya. 'An ancient contraption containing a wormhole in time. You never know what will show up when it's activated, but it's rarely something good.' She turned to find Mr Kamel, her grandfather's genie butler. 'Travellers have used it to round up rogues for hundreds of years. But if you're wondering whose idea it was to use it to practise rusty SWAT skills . . . well, it wasn't mine.' Kamel replaced the thin wire glasses he had been polishing on to his thin nose. Like always, he was dressed from head to toe in tweed. 'But you know your grandfather. Once he decides on something, there's no stopping him.'

Aliya looked from Kamel to her grandfather in surprise. Ever since the summer, when Dorian Darke had reappeared to wreak havoc on the *Silver Express*, Geddo had talked about putting his team together again. Aliya had thought it had been nothing but talk. Partly because Geddo was unwell, but also because most of the Brigade members had long been retired. They had grown old. This had to be a sign that her grandfather really was better than he looked, and that the Brigade still were a force to be reckoned with, which was a good thing. Although she would have preferred if he left possibly illegal traps full of dangerous creatures out of the equation.

Now Geddo turned to his sister, Aliya's great-aunt Gigi, who stood next to him looking flamboyant in a fur stole and pillbox hat. 'Press the button, Gigi.'

'I've just had a manicure,' Gigi said, holding up her nails to show him. 'Olfat can do it.'

Taking the box, the ghoul hostel matron gave its button a firm whack. An instant later, the pygmy goblins were caught, as if by a strong wind, which carried them towards the Pandora Box.

Aliya followed Jax's pursuit of the last pygmy, which was struggling against the box's pull. It eventually disappeared inside, still grasping something white and hairy in its fist.

'It took my toupee!' Jax cried, gesticulating.

'Never mind,' the ghoul matron said. 'I'll give you a hair pudding.'

'That makes hair grow *everywhere*. I'd rather not have hairy elbows, if you don't mind.'

Over in a corner Aliya spotted Mercuria Mellow, the Brigade's crisis negotiator, snoozing in an armchair. She looked like an old turtle. Next to her, Jalaluddin Saria, their chief navigator, was drinking a glass of milk with great concentration.

'Jalaluddin's got acid reflux,' Kamel explained. 'And Mercuria takes a nap at this time every day, after lunch. Helps with the digestion.' He gestured vaguely at his stomach.

Aliya watched in disbelief as a squabble broke out between Jax and Jalaluddin over the last fuul sandwich on the snack cart.

'Are they always like this?' she asked Kamel.

'A long time ago, when they raided the Shop of Second Chances, Dorian hit them with a squabble curse. Maybe that's why they can't stop bickering, even now. Some say that's why they disbanded, but they won't admit it. They squabble about that too. But whether it's the curse or just bad tempers or old age, if a pod can't get along and trust each other, they're doomed.'

Aliya thought of her own pod's quarrel over lunch. It was true that they'd grown a bit distant these past few weeks, but they would surely never turn into this.

'Is this such a great idea?' Aliya asked her grandfather when training was over and they were having bitter lemonade with mint. The dungeon was calm now. The Pandora Box had been safely tucked away and Jalaluddin and Jax had taken their squabbling elsewhere. Mercuria had left to feed her cats. Only Geddo, Great-Aunt Gigi, Mr Kamel and Matron remained with Aliya.

'I wanted you to see the state of things,' Geddo said. 'I'm doing what I can to protect you and the city, as is my duty, but as you can see –' he winced, touching the side of his belly where the wound was – 'we're hardly a force to be reckoned with, with some exceptions.' He nodded at Mr Kamel and Matron, who sat silently watching him.

'Last time I saw Dorian, on the train, he was really weak,' Aliya said. 'I doubt he'll be back. Even if he tried, I don't think he can do much in his state, and there's Prickly, isn't there? And all these security upgrades he's done to keep magic out of the Infinitum?'

She couldn't tell him what she had seen that morning. Besides, it must have been her mind playing tricks with her. She was becoming more and more convinced that she couldn't have seen the Darkling.

'You know better than anyone that the security forces can't be relied on when it comes to fighting magic,' Geddo said. 'We're lucky if Prickly manages to keep himself out of trouble.'

Aliya knew what he was referring to. Only last night, they had seen the inspector chasing one of his security robots down their street, frantically blowing his whistle. Prickly's constant mishaps with the new robotic patrol the Council had insisted he use had become a steady source of amusement to the Citadel, and a great embarrassment to his daughter.

'Something bad is coming,' Geddo continued. 'There are whispers, new cracks in the atmosphere.'

'You really are making too much of these vague rumours.' Great-Aunt Gigi put her cup of Turkish coffee down. 'Sultan Junior must focus on what lies ahead! Her pod is trying out to be Sweepers tonight. That's what's important!'

'What's important, Gigi, is that my only grandchild is *safe*.' Geddo gave her a thunderous look.

'The Great Race is a wonderful opportunity to cut one's teeth at being a real traveller.' Gigi brushed an invisible speck of dust from Aliya's shoulder. 'She'll make us all proud, and it will look very good on her record.'

Pride was a big thing with Great-Aunt Gigi and now, like every time Aliya met her, she felt the weight of the Sultan family legacy on her shoulders. Since Aliya had joined the travel community, a tug of war had existed between her great-aunt and her grandfather. While Gigi tried to make her responsible for the family's legacy, Geddo tried to free her from it, all to keep her safe.

'Last summer I sent you away on that train

thinking you'd be safer,' Geddo grumbled, with a pained expression. 'But see where that got us. This . . . race. It's not a good idea for you to try out.'

'But it's a matter of honour.' Aliya looked from her great-aunt to her grandfather. She and the pod had been training for *weeks*. There was no way she could pull out. 'Once you've signed up, there's no backing down.'

'Precisely so. I'm her guardian too, remember?' Gigi agreed. 'And I say she must join.'

Geddo sighed heavily.

'Then it's on your head if your hankering for Sultan glory gets her killed.'

Gigi threw up her hands. 'Yaa! Old age has certainly made you dramatic!'

'He's doing his best,' Mr Kamel said when he escorted Aliya back up the spiralling staircase, leaving the squabbling elders behind. 'Your grandfather cares about one thing in this world, and that is keeping you safe. Got that way after your parents were murdered. He thinks he failed them, that he should've *been there*. Still, you've got to do what you've got to do.' Kamel held out a hand to steady her as the stair circled. 'I've always thought he was overprotective, but then we genies don't share your ideas about child-rearing. I was thrown in a snake pit by my mother at the age of five. The venom does wonders for the hair. Have you ever seen a bald genie?'

Aliya shook her head. She had seen genies change colour, go invisible and walk around without their heads, but the hair thing was true. Maybe she should tell Jax Jaxson.

'Why didn't you say something?' she asked. 'If you thought he was overprotective?'

'Not my place to interfere.' Kamel paused. 'And there's another thing no one can protect you from.' He laid a hand on her shoulder. 'You must know that your grandfather is dying.'

They stood silently for some moments, letting her take this in. The staircase slowly circled upwards. Suddenly Aliya felt everything spinning, both inside of her and out. She clung to the banister. But when they reached the top and the staircase stopped moving, she turned to Kamel.

'You're wrong,' she whispered. 'He'll be fine. I'll make sure of it.'

Kamel looked at her for a moment with grave, concerned eyes.

'I know that's what you want to believe, but—'

She held a hand up to dismiss his words. 'I'll find a way. I swear to you.'

'You don't have to swear to me.'

'Then I'll swear it to myself.'

Kamel gave her a quick squeeze and a pat on the cheek before leaving her, standing at the top of the stairs, still feeling like she was spinning.

It was later, when Aliya was alone in her and Karima's room after classes, that she noticed it for the first time – a small black spot on Simi's orange chest, near her heart. For a moment, she imagined that her own feelings, because of what Kamel had said about Geddo, were manifesting on the nadim. Because what other colour could contain the thought of one's grandfather dying? Nadims were like a physical manifestation of their locksmith's spirits, so she guessed it would be possible.

All through that afternoon's classes, and during dinner, she had sat as if in a bubble, hardly hearing what anyone around her was saying. Inside her, however, everything was *loud*. Every feeling, every thought blasted through her, like explosion after explosion, her head ringing with pain.

Karima had noticed, of course. Perhaps she had known about Geddo's state already. She'd not seemed surprised when Aliya told her what Kamel had said. Throughout the afternoon, she'd been at Aliya's side, feeding her remedies to soften the blow to her heart. Bottled lightning for the shock, camel tears for the grief, and Roc bird droppings to ease her nausea.

'I'm so sorry,' Karima said as they got ready to leave for the try-outs. She had paused trying to squirm her way into the smartsuit Aion had left, and stood looking at Aliya, her curly hair framed by the moonlight that shone through the mirror, illuminating it like a halo. 'I wish there was something I could do.'

Aliya stared at her. Karima too had given up on Geddo, just like Kamel. Throughout the day, Aliya's sadness had been building into frustration. Now she felt a sudden rush of anger.

'If you wanted to help, why'd you stop developing an antidote like you promised? I guess you found more important things to do.'

Karima looked stunned.

'Because now you're suddenly nowhere to be found,' Aliya went on. 'Always away, doing . . . Actually, I have no idea, cos you don't tell me, do you? I guess it's some secret project I'm not special enough to know about.'

Karima had always been too busy. It had been like that ever since they had become friends. She was always getting caught up in things, usually to do with her menacin. She had always been a workaholic, but when they were trying to develop a cure for Geddo, they had at least done it together. Now her friend had added secrecy to the list of friendship challenges.

'I wish I could tell you what I'm working on,' Karima said after a pause. 'But I promised I wouldn't.'

'Oh,' Aliya said and thought: *So now she has secrets with someone else.* Everyone had secrets these days, it seemed. She was getting sick of them.

'About the antidote,' Karima continued, looking stricken. 'Even Matron said it was no use trying any more. That we must accept that—'

'It was *no use* trying to save my grandpa?'

'That's not what I meant.'

Aliya turned to grab her suit from the bed.

'I don't care what you *meant*,' she snapped. 'What does that help?'

'I-I really don't know what you expected me to do,' Karima whispered. 'We tried our best. We worked on that antidote for *weeks* and—'

'Well, you could've tried harder,' Aliya cut her off. 'You could've not given up. *I'm* not giving up. I'm never giving up.'

She sat heavily on the bed, staring at her feet. Out of the corner of her eye she saw Karima disappear into the bathroom and shut the door behind her.

Chapter 5
THE TRY-OUTS

Aliya had never before set foot in the Infinitum Archives. It was a place surrounded by strange tales, often told around the fireplace in the hostel common rooms. The archives held records from every single time trip taken since the very beginnings of the Infinitum, and were therefore older than most of the travellers. Like the Smithy, it was not just a place, but an enigma. Some of the cabinets had been made from ancient trees out of the Wilderness – the unchartered part of the Infinitum that lay beyond the boundaries of the Citadel. Although stripped of its magic, the wood was unpredictable. Some cabinets were even said to contain unregistered portals from the time before the Infinitum administration got organized.

Aliya and her pod's only connection to the archives was through Edith, a Victorian in their grade who was apprenticed to Mr Blot, the chief archivist. As far as Aliya knew, Edith hadn't got into any dangerous trouble since she'd started her menteeship, apart from developing a dust allergy. Still, the news that it had been chosen as the location for this year's try-outs had filled the pod with trepidation. Their job during the trial would be to locate and close whatever portal they found open, and in such a place as the archives, with all those cabinets, the task seemed daunting.

Aliya and Victoria stood huddling on the archive steps, waiting to be let in. There was an hour left until the event began and, around them, the rest of the competitors had begun to gather. A few steps down, Karima stood talking with Aion and Fuad. After their fight earlier in the evening, Karima and Aliya hadn't spoken. Several times on their way to the archives, Aliya had tried to approach the subject, at least in her own mind, but something stopped her. It was all too much, too chaotic. She didn't know how to untangle what she felt. The only thing she knew with absolute certainty – the thing that would solve all others – was that she needed to find an antidote to save her grandfather's life.

Aliya glanced down at Karima, hoping to catch her eye, but she was helping to adjust something on Fuad's smartsuit. After much convincing, Victoria had accepted that they'd all wear the suits during the try-outs in the hope that they would increase their chances of winning. The smartclothes were made of a thin, breathable material that Aion had developed by recycling the futuristic sheets her parents had sent her to use during term. Fabrics that detected your needs were a staple in her native time of the 2090s.

Aliya lifted Simi down from her shoulder and stroked her across the back. She had tied a thin cord around her right leg that connected to her wrist, to prevent her from flying off. Aliya's eyes again fell on the black spot on the nadim's chest – was it really a reflection of her own mood, or did it mean something more sinister?

'It's really not fair,' Victoria started. 'Edith's been

helping the pods from Hippolyta's, drawing them maps and everything.' She nodded towards the pods that stood on the steps some way off. Aliya counted four of them – all competing to sweep for the Hippolyta's senior race pod, the Philosophers. Luckily, Aliya's pod would only have to compete against the Nepos for the chance to sweep for the Ghoulies. The rules dictated that Sweepers only competed against their own hostels. Nevertheless, Victoria was upset at the others' advantages. She didn't like anyone outshining her.

'And the Mehmet pods have been drilled by the Janissaries, of course,' she went on. 'They're like machines. Thank God we're not competing against them.' Victoria turned the other way to glare at groups of second- and third-graders in the tell-tale turbans of the Mehmet Nazim Hostel.

'We're up last,' said Mustafa, who had just returned from the secretariat, waving a slip of paper.

'Something good at least,' Victoria said. 'We'll watch and avoid the others' mistakes.'

'That's the thing.' Mustafa looked anxious. 'This year each pod gets a different challenge.'

'What?' Aliya and Victoria cried in unison. All the years previous, the Council had only created one type of trial, usually in line with what the juniors had practised in their classes. It could be false portals that opened to dead ends, or portals that refused to be closed and needed skill to be overpowered.

At that moment, the big doors of the archives began to open.

'What's that?' Aliya pointed at a small, fluffy thing in Mustafa's hands. He showed her. It was a key ring in the shape of a rabbit with a unicorn horn. When Mustafa stroked it across the back, it made a nibbling sound, clacking its small teeth together.

'It's a miraj,' he said. 'They're selling them in the gift shop over at the Refuge. Thought it'd give us luck. Not exactly a rabbit's foot, but still. It's silly, I know.' He threw a glance over his shoulder. 'You haven't seen any hieracosphinxes around, have you?'

They were interrupted by a team of shuffler robots, the kind of AI humanoids that the Infinitum Traffic Department used to conduct traffic, or farmers used to herd cattle in the green belt between the

Citadel and the Wilderness.

'Charming,' Fuad muttered as a shuffler poked him repeatedly on his behind to make him move along. Together with the other competitors, the pod was brought through a darkened passage. At the end, Aliya could see a rectangle of light – the doorway to the inner archives.

Once inside, Aliya and the rest of the students stood, open-mouthed, gazing around them. Before them lay a large circular space, like a circus ring, around which seemingly endless rows of cabinets sat. Between them Aliya could discern dimly lit aisles. Some of the cabinets looked ancient, as though fashioned out of the trunks of wild, old trees, with leafy branches still sticking out here and there, some still holding berries or apples.

But more remarkable were the large wooden cabinets that were bobbing in the air above them. They had been made to float sideways to accommodate the Council jury and the audience, all peering down at them. The space was lit by softly glowing lanterns – orbs that floated like oversized fireflies in mid-air.

Aliya's locksmith peers had been working for

weeks at the archives and had been very secretive about what they were doing. *So that's what it was about*, she thought, gazing up at the gravity-defying storage. *Vitalizing cabinets to float.*

Just then, a flurry of leatherbound books zoomed in, their pages rustling as they swooshed in orchestrated patterns through the air above the arena. Picking up speed, they shot over the heads of the seated audience, some pausing to snap at hats. This fancy book-flying show was no doubt the brainchild of her fellow apprentice, Omar Sadik. He was always making things fly at the Smithy. Once he had made some tableware from the Smithy's cafeteria chase her down a corridor and squirt coffee at her. *Show-off*, she thought.

Some of the cabinets carried students come to cheer for their hostel's pods. The Mehmet supporters were easy to spot with their serious demeanour and turbans. The Hippolyta scholars lounged on another cabinet, as easy-going as the Mehmets were stern. In their midst sat their matron, Madame Hippolyta, a lady with big hair and dangly necklaces. Her bejewelled arms were draped protectively over the shoulders of the two students nearest to her.

On top of their own hostel's cabinet sat Mrs Dickens and Esmat, Great-Aunt Gigi's genie assistant. Next to them, the Ghoulie race pod held banners with the Khedivial crest and star. Aliya hoped they were there to cheer for them too, not just the Nepos.

Her heart pinched as she spotted her grandfather on top of a floating oak cabinet, sunk into an armchair, his old eyes magnified by a pair of thick glasses, the ones he wore to watch television. He looked so small, so shrunken, as if he were turning into a human raisin. Great-Aunt Gigi was there too, looking stately in a velvet gown with neck ruffles.

'Oh, look, there's Papa,' Fuad said and pointed. Mr Mandil was waving at them excitedly.

Mrs Mandil, a small lady in a cloche hat, had her hand to her mouth in a gesture of contained terror. The twins' mother was not a traveller herself, and Mr Mandil was a dud, a portal-keeper. The floating cabinets, the frolicking books . . . it was a bit much, Aliya supposed, for someone not used to the travel world and its eccentricities.

'Are your parents here?' Aliya asked Aion.

'Depends on how you define *here*,' Aion said, pointing upwards to where a bearded man and a lady in a sparkly silver dress sat cross-legged in mid-air.

'Attending holographically again, are they?' Aliya asked.

Aion shrugged in reply. Her parents' constant absence was a sore topic.

Some members of the Infinitum Council sat on a floating cabinet at the centre, facing the audience. Aliya hardly knew any of their names. One she definitely recognized was Neon Ticker, the Council spokesperson, who now stood up and spread his arms in a welcoming gesture. He was dressed in a deep-purple kaftan, embroidered with gold. Although it was a traditional garment, there was something about the cut and the lines of the sleeves that made it look modern, which perfectly matched his new hairstyle. His lilac hair was combed back and accentuated by sharp sideburns.

'Welcome to Sweeper try-outs for the Great Race,' he began, smiling widely, first at the audience and then at the genie and pixie news team that hovered nearby on a floating carpet. 'As you know, every two years we invite those younger travellers who seek an additional challenge and a chance at glory to try out as Sweepers. These pods follow the competing seniors to close the portals they open. This year, we're doing things a little bit differently. Mr Blot and I have designed a truly unique challenge for your entertainment.' Here, he gestured at Mr Blot, a tall man who sat alone on top of a floating book cart. His bald head glinted in the light. He was wearing a mouse-brown cardigan and had a feather duster tucked under one arm. Aliya knew that it was an anti-magic wand in disguise. Unlike most of the senior staff at the Infinitum, Mr Blot took the threat of magic seriously. Maybe because many of his older cabinets had been made out of once-enchanted trees which, although they had been stripped of their magic, were still full of mischief.

'If something goes wrong tonight, it's on your head!' Neon shouted at him. Turning to the cameras, he said, 'I'm joking, of course.'

Mr Blot stood up. He bowed stiffly at the Council, then looked down at the assembled students.

'All right, listen up, you lot,' he said in a broad cockney accent. 'This is 'ow it works. One pod at a time enters the arena. The rest of ya stay put over there.'

He pointed at what looked like a big birdcage. Edith, the archive apprentice, stood holding the door open. Aliya noticed that she too wore a mouse-brown cardigan and had a feather duster tucked under her arm.

'You lot,' she parroted. 'Get moving . . . if you please.'

'Is he going to put us in a cage?' Victoria scowled. 'What are we? Budgies?'

Victoria gestured up at her father, the inspector, who stared back at her, brow furrowed. Victoria was forever trying to play the daddy card, but Aliya couldn't remember him ever giving his daughter special treatment. He was fair in that way, the inspector.

'Edith says Blot uses the cage to trap the rogue things that sometimes slip out of the cabinets,' Mustafa said as they shuffled forward. 'And travellers who don't submit their mission reports on time. But I think that one was a joke.'

'Things . . . like what?' Aliya asked.

Mustafa gave her an anxious look.

'She didn't want to tell me.'

With the shuffler robots prodding them, the students moved, herd-like, into the great cage, where benches had been arranged for them. All except the first pod from Mehmet's Hostel, who headed to the centre of the arena.

'Now, I ask that all onlookers remain seated at all times,' Neon Ticker said. 'You will be able to follow the events right there.'

He pointed to a huge carpet that had swooped out from the shadows and hung in mid-air above the centre of the arena. As the carpet unfurled, Aliya could see that it was completely white. Words appeared, reading: *Welcome to the Sweeper try-outs*.

'Strap yourselves in with the seat belts provided,' Neon instructed the audience.

Aliya looked up to see Matron Olfat strapping Geddo into his armchair with a snap-n-lock buckle. She felt tension creeping up on her. What kind of trial would this turn out to be if it needed seat belts?

'Now, remember,' Neon continued, 'no one is to move from their seats, no matter what happens! Let the first trial begin!'

A great swooshing noise accompanied his last word. A gust of wind rushed through the stacks of books and wooden cabinets and burst into the arena at ground level. The wind carried with it a great mass of papers that swept in over the audience and the waiting pods like a flock of white birds. It spun around them with a high-pitched *wheeee*, making Aliya feel as if she might fall off her seat.

'It's a trixie wind,' Fuad cried excitedly next to her. 'They've really taken things to another level this year.'

Aliya grasped the wood of the bench with both hands. Trixie winds, she knew, could change direction at any moment and blow you off your feet in a fraction of a second.

'*Our first pod comes from Mehmet Nazim's Hostel in the Ottoman Quarter,*' Neon narrated through a speaker. '*Somewhere in the archives there is an open portal through which the wind is coming. Will the pod be able to close it in time? Start the timer, Zandra!*'

Next to him, a greenish genie in a silver suit turned over a large hourglass, setting a fine stream of sand in motion.

The screen now showed the pod running through a narrow aisle lined by cabinets. The leader, a boy called Tareq, was holding up a golden stick.

'A portal sensor,' Victoria sniffed. 'How basic.'

Suddenly, the wind caught up with the pod, lifted them off the floor, and swirled them about. But the group quickly caught on and began using swimming strokes in the air to get out of the current. Moments later, they were steady on their feet again and had located the source of the wind – a green cupboard at the end of aisle 53 B. Flat on his belly to avoid the blasting wind, Tareq hauled out his travel key and lunged at the keyhole. He turned the key anti-clockwise and – *click*. The portal closed. The archives quieted. Flying papers drifted to the floor like snow. On the screen, Zandra held up the hourglass. Only half the time had passed. A cheer went up from the audience.

'*Our first pod has passed with flying colours,*' Neon announced. '*Let's show them our appreciation.*'

The great hall thundered with applause.

Next was one of the Hippolyta pods, who had to discern a real portal among a number of fake ones. They managed this by using aura crystals, which could detect falsehood by sensing the energy of a thing. Aliya watched breathlessly as the Hippolyta navigator read the auras of the cabinet doors by passing her crystal over them. Some turned the gems brown which, Victoria explained, meant the portals were fake. When they reached the right one – an old cabinet that was still part apple tree – the crystal turned a startling green.

The rest of the pods passed in quick succession, all successful and only varying in how fast they had been. And then it was time for the two Olfat pods, the final showdown to end the evening. The Nepos passed without much fuss. Their portal did give them some trouble by moving between different locations in the same aisle. Their time was fast, but Aliya's pod agreed it was beatable, which didn't stop Victoria having a final grumble.

'That was too easy,' she said, glaring up at Francesca Flux on the screen. 'I'd bet my front teeth that she's pulled some strings. *Nepotism.*'

Then it was their turn to walk out of the birdcage and enter the arena. Aliya glanced up at Geddo, who stared back at her. His glasses magnified his eyes so much that it was impossible to read the rest of his expression. Next to him, Great-Aunt Gigi gave her a tearful look that was at once proud and full of expectation. Aliya knew it to mean: *You are a Sultan! Don't let us down.*

'*It is time for our last pod to show us what they're made of,*' Neon announced. '*And, please, a final reminder to stay in your seats, no matter what happens.*'

Aliya thought this last remark sounded menacing, almost like a threat, but decided it was her tension talking.

'Remember what we've practised,' Victoria said as they huddled together. 'This is our chance to prove to our parents that we *can* do this and that we belong here.' The pod nodded in agreement.

'Activate smartsuits,' Fuad whispered, and they all touched small buttons on their chests. Aliya could feel the suit whirring against her body, cool and sleek, like an extra layer of skin. Above them the audience *oooh*ed in admiration. This was a good start. They were the only team who'd worn anything like the suits – the pods were allowed to bring any equipment they could think of or manage to invent. That was part of the challenge: to be creative and think outside the box.

'Come on then, stake out the area,' Victoria whispered, looking pleased. 'Look for portals. Regroup and report. And –' Victoria turned to Aliya – '*control your bird.*'

'She's not a bird—' Aliya began, but the lights suddenly went out, plunging the whole archive into darkness. For a few seconds, the pod stood in silence.

'Is this part of it?' Mustafa's voice came through the dark. 'Is this the trial?'

As if in answer, the image of the hourglass appeared on the big screen above them, the thin stream of sand shining silver, the only bright thing in the blackness.

'Darkness?' Victoria said. 'No one's ever got darkness before.'

'I told you they're playing at a different level this year,' Fuad said. 'Aion, what have we got that could illuminate the space?'

'That's easy. Our suits,' Aion said. A moment later they stood in a circle of warm light, their smart-suits glowing with a thousand little lights merged into the fabric. Now, at least, they could see each other and some of what was around them, but beyond that the blackness was thick, almost like something alive. Aliya felt fear come creeping.

'I don't like this,' Mustafa said in a small voice, echoing Aliya's trepidation.

'Come on,' Karima said. 'Our *parents* are up there.' She gestured upwards where, right now, there was only a thick curtain of darkness. 'Nothing bad can happen.'

Aliya exhaled. Karima was right. Just because the darkness felt sinister, didn't mean it was. This was a test set by the Infinitum Council, after all.

'The darkness is the clue,' she said. 'Think about it. Whatever changes in the atmosphere comes out of the portal we're supposed to close.'

'But how do we find it?' Karima asked, avoiding

looking at Aliya. There was an edge in her voice. Aliya ignored it.

Victoria rummaged through her satchel. 'We'll just have to use the night-time navigation protocol. Put these on.' She handed out what looked like swim goggles. 'For night vision.'

Once on, the goggles turned everything a hazy green, but Aliya could see their surroundings again. Above them, the cabinets hovered, and to the right was the big hourglass. One quarter of it had already seeped away.

'I hate to say it,' Victoria continued, 'but the fastest way would be to use Mustafa's insect.'

'Really?' Mustafa, brightening, reached into an inner pocket and brought out a scarab beetle. The insect was about as big as an unshelled walnut. Its black body had an oily sheen that reflected all the colours of the rainbow. Bahiti was an ancient species of Egyptian beetle, and her minute antennae could detect changes in the atmosphere, including the special energy emitted by portals. Mustafa had spent months training her to home in on portal energy, but this was the first time Victoria had accepted her help.

'All right, darling.' Mustafa stroked the beetle gently over her sleek back. 'Do your thing.'

In the light of the smartsuits, the scarab whirred into action, her sheer wings lifting her tubby body off Mustafa's palm. 'She's sensing it,' he cried. 'Come on!'

They ran between the dark stacks, following Bahiti, who buzzed ahead. As they reached the end of one of the narrow aisles between the archive cabinets, the darkness deepened, flowing towards them in waves, like thick soup.

'Not far now.' Mustafa pointed at the scarab, who was zooming ahead of them with surprising speed for something so small. The pod followed, turning around the last cabinet and into another aisle, where the darkness felt thick enough to cut with a knife. And then, there it was – an old green cabinet at the end of the aisle. The portal.

'Karima,' Victoria hollered. 'This is you! Get your key out and close this dastardly thing!'

In the faint light emitted by their smartsuits, Aliya watched as Karima pulled out her key and moved closer to the portal. Her key blade, with its golden retriever handle, began to radiate as she searched for the keyhole.

'I can't find it!' Karima cried. 'Something's wrong!'

'You're just not aiming correctly!' Victoria pushed forward, grabbing Karima by the wrist.

Something was moving behind them in the darkness. Aliya heard Mustafa scream. Turning, she saw shadowy hands and arms grabbing at him. There were beings there in the dark! Now they were clutching at Aion, trying to pull her into a cupboard.

No! Aliya struggled. On her right shoulder she sensed her nadim heating up, brightening, then felt her locksmith power pool into her palms. It all happened in seconds. Lunging forward, she swiped at the shadow that held the struggling Mustafa, her hands like glowing firebrands. The shadow receded. Aliya continued swiping around her, her hands leaving bright traces in the dark. Just seeing the Baraka was enough to deter the other shadows too, because they withdrew.

'What was that?' Aliya panted when they were huddling together again.

'It's like the dark came alive.' Mustafa was hugging himself. 'I went all cold when it touched me. It was *awful*.'

'It was probably one of the senior pods,' Victoria spat. 'Some dratted prank to make us lose focus!'

'Or something came out of one of the rogue portals,' Karima whispered.

'I-I can't do this—' Mustafa began, but Victoria grabbed him by both arms and shook him.

'We haven't got *time* for pranks!' she shouted. 'And I don't care if half the Wilderness comes through that portal. We're going to *do* this!'

Simi, who sat perched on Aliya's shoulder, suddenly gave a loud cry. Before she could react, the nadim had shot towards the open portal.

'Simi,' Aliya breathed, lunging after her. Simi was hovering like a hummingbird, just at the portal's opening. The sight gave Aliya an uncanny déjà vu. This was just what had happened that morning in the Smithy.

For some moments, the nadim was swallowed by the darkness. Aliya frantically groped for her, moving closer and closer.

Then she saw it: black scales slipping past the opening, moving inside the cupboard. The great snake head. The Darkling was there.

Now Aliya felt the tug and the pull of magic hauling her in, sucking at her like an undercurrent beneath her terror. Suddenly, she too longed to go to the Darkling, to plunge through and lose herself in its coils. This wasn't a prank. Someone had opened a portal to the Shop of Second Chances here, in the middle of the Citadel, and she was being drawn into it.

Mesmerized, Aliya moved towards the snake. One hand sank into the darkness on the other side when—

Smack.

'What are you doing?' Victoria shouted at her. 'Didn't I tell you to control your bird?'

Aliya woke as if from a trance. Victoria had slapped her right across the cheek.

Reaching out, Aliya quickly plucked Simi out of the air. The nadim uttered a fierce, affronted screech, but Aliya had no time to consider her now. She had to close this portal – fast.

Giving Simi a firm stroke over her crest, she felt

her transform into a key. Aliya closed her eyes, mustering all the locksmith powers her panic-stricken brain could summon. Locksmiths didn't need specially prepared keyholes to open portals – they could make them anywhere. But to *close* it, she *would* need one, and she couldn't find it. There was one more option. She could shut this rogue portal by opening another one in its stead, a technique called 'overriding'. She'd learnt about it with Nigm, but had never tried it.

Sliding Simi along the edge of the doorway, she saw the tell-tale pulse of light. Moments later, the darkness gave way to a shimmering glow. The aisle around them brightened and Aliya let out a relieved breath. She had done it. She had blocked the evil. Around them, the darkness cleared. The archives brightened as the glowing orb lamps lit up once more.

'What just happened?' Karima said, her voice trembling.

Aliya shook her head.

'I don't know,' she lied. 'Some kind of glitch, maybe.'

She couldn't tell them what she feared – that Simi

had somehow opened yet another portal into the Shop of Second Chances. But the nadim had not even been in her key shape when it happened. And what about those figures in the darkness that had tried to catch them? Had they really been the seniors playing a prank, or some old cabinet playing up? Or had it been something more sinister, something released from a dangerous portal opened on purpose?

'Our time is up,' Victoria screeched behind her.

Aliya looked up at the great hourglass that hovered above them on the screen. The last grains of sand were just emptying into the bottom half.

'Did we make it?' Fuad called from down the aisle. 'Did we close the portal?'

'I don't think so,' Mustafa said, cradling Bahiti in his palm. 'Look.'

Something was emerging backwards out of the portal Aliya had opened, something small and fluffy. Aliya blinked. She had meant to open a portal to the hostel common room, but what was this? As the little creature turned, she saw that it was a small, brown rabbit. A thin, pinkish horn shot out of its forehead.

'It's a miraj!' Mustafa exclaimed. 'She's opened a portal to the Refuge! To the miraj enclosure!'

The Refuge, where Mustafa worked with mythical creatures, had species that were kept apart because of their wildness. Mirajes were one such breed. Aliya looked down at her hands, which were still glowing with Baraka energy. Seeing Mustafa's rabbit key chain had somehow made her mess things up again. She was *hopeless*.

'Look, there're more of them!' Karima cried. What began as a trickle of horned rabbits was turning into a deluge.

'*It looks like our last pod is having some difficulties,*' Neon's voice rang out above them. '*Their locksmith, currently the youngest apprentice at the Smithy, seems to be in trouble again . . . Oh dear.*'

The mirajes were pouring into the archives now, jumping down the corridors, bouncing off the walls and into shelves and open cupboards, where they began tearing manuscripts to pieces with their sharp, nibbling teeth. Aliya watched, stunned, as the small unicorn rabbits gnawed at the lower edge of the carpet screen. They were cute and destructive in equal measure. Mr Blot and Edith were trying to herd them into some kind of order with the help of the shuffler robots.

'Everything is *lost!*' Victoria roared, falling to her knees, mirajes tumbling over her. 'We're *done for!*'

Aliya bit her lip. Failing respectably would have been fine – they were the youngest competitors after all. But Victoria was right – Aliya's error had made a spectacle of them. By opening a portal to the Refuge, she'd ruined everything. Simi, who had been fluttering around her, now alighted on Aliya's hand. Stroking her chest, Aliya had another shock. The black spot had grown into a large ink blob across her breast. Simi was turning black.

'It's not that bad,' Karima tried, patting Victoria on the back.

'Not that bad?' Victoria hollered. 'We'll be scrutinized, probably disbanded. We've lost our chance to be real travellers.'

Aliya looked straight ahead, trying to keep apart. She just couldn't face Victoria now, or herself, or grasp what it was that was happening to her and to Simi.

Mustafa had joined Mr Blot, Edith, and the

shuffler robots' attempts to herd the mirajes back through the portal. Above them, agitated voices grew in volume.

'Just keep calm,' Neon's voice echoed through the speakers. *'We'll soon know more.'*

'What are they saying?' Victoria cried. 'Will they give us another chance because she *sabotaged* us?' She pointed an accusing finger at Aliya. 'She let her bird fly off and—'

'They're not talking about us,' Fuad interrupted, pointing at the screen. 'Look.'

The carpet screen was showing the light-green pixie reporter who had accosted Aliya that morning, standing outside the golden door at Qahira Square – the door that led to the Smithy. At first, Aliya's mind struggled to take in what she was saying. She heard the words 'locksmiths', 'disappeared' and 'suspicion'.

'That can't be right,' Fuad said.

'What?' Aliya asked, frowning.

'Didn't you hear? The locksmiths all disappeared while creating the racecourse.'

He looked up at the screen again.

'Could it really be as bad as that?' the pixie reporter

was saying. *'Could our locksmiths, the ones we've come to trust to keep our world together, be the ones seeking its destruction? Why else would they disappear without a trace and abandon us just as our world begins to crack apart once again?'*

The reporter pointed upwards, the camera following. There was a rift in the very texture of the sky, running like a huge claw mark down to the ground. *'Rather than protecting us, could they be plotting our world's end? Have we been fooled all along?'* She looked gravely into the camera. *'We accepted their secrecy, believing they were working for our benefit, but perhaps our trust was the very thing allowing them to plot against us.'*

Mustafa shook his head.

'This doesn't make any sense at all.'

'What?' Aliya breathed.

Mustafa pointed to the screen again, now showing an angry crowd that had gathered outside the golden door that led to the Smithy. Red letters had been painted across it, reading:

Traitors.

Chapter 6
NEON VISITS

It was past midnight. The commotion that had followed the news of the missing locksmiths had finally died down and the city had sunk into a fretful slumber. At Matron Olfat's Scholastic Hostel, Aliya's pod had crawled off to bed, exhausted, sad, with ears still ringing from the mix of lectures and consolation their parents had given them after the failed try-outs.

But Aliya could not sleep. Once the others had left, she had remained sitting by the common room fire Mrs Dickens had made for them. On the table in front of her, the cook had left a heap of soul-comforting goodies to ease the sting of failure. But for Aliya it wasn't just the spectacular defeat at the try-outs that stung. The locksmiths, including her mentor Professor Nigm, had vanished. The whole Citadel was whispering about them and about the strange cracks that were appearing all over the city again, cracks that the locksmiths should have been mending. As she and her pod had made their way home from the try-outs, the whispers had been everywhere, spreading like wildfire:

'. . . always keeping themselves apart in that strange workshop. That's suspicious – if anything . . .'

'. . . should've been made to show us what they're up to in that place . . .'

'. . . think they're so special . . .'

Aliya had hoped to spend the evening with Geddo, but attending the try-outs had exhausted him. After patting her on the head and telling her not to worry, he had been carted off on a flying carpet by a band of ghoul maids and put promptly to bed. Mr Kamel and the other adults had taken off too, to find out more about the missing locksmiths, so the children had been left to their own devices. Great-Aunt Gigi had been particularly dramatic about the failure and Aliya had been grateful when her genie assistant, Esmat, had bundled her into a departing whizzcalator. Simi had not been much comfort either, what with her odd behaviour and growing black spot. Just looking at her made Aliya's stomach knot with worry. It was as though the Darkling was tainting Simi more and more with each encounter.

Why, Aliya thought again, *did I feel drawn to the Darkling?* With the thought came another surge of desperation. What if it meant that she and Simi were being drawn into the magic and becoming cursed? Maybe that was her fate. Did she have a 'tendency' to be drawn to the dark side, like Arsinoe had claimed many locksmiths did? But to work with the Sublimes, one needed to be pure, because they could sense a person, read them. She had experienced it herself. Perhaps the tendency Arsinoe was talking about was something else. Maybe it was a hunger that grew within the locksmiths, ignited by their closeness to the Sublimes – a hunger for power. Maybe their special status really did go to their heads and had made them forget their origins. Magic was just the next, natural step . . . This had been the evolution of Dorian Darke, as Geddo had explained to her. She had never wanted to believe that it could be equally true for other locksmiths.

She stroked the hoopoe's back tenderly. The nadim uttered a soft croak and looked at her sideways through its intelligent black eye.

The sound of a knock interrupted Aliya's gloom.

She looked around the messy common room. Strewn over the Persian rugs and the armchairs were a potpourri of her podmates' belongings: Aion's odd bits of tech and abandoned projects (a robotic sausage-dog vacuum cleaner stood parked in a corner); Victoria's maps lying mixed with Mustafa's Roc-bird treats.

Aliya was about to walk over to the door when the knock came again – from the window. She cautiously pulled it open.

Neon Ticker stood outside, smiling. Aliya frowned in surprise, because the window, which should have overlooked the hostel courtyard, now led to a finely furnished room.

'Council-approved shortcut,' Neon explained, gesturing at the room behind him. 'Would you step into my office?'

'How . . . how did you know I was awake?' was all Aliya could think of to say. She had never been this close to Neon Ticker, never mind spoken to him. Still, she felt as though she knew him. He was always on the news, or a guest on Infinitum talk shows. As he offered his hand, Aliya was struck by how flawless he looked, with his white skin and lilac hair. Up close, he almost didn't look real.

'A lucky guess,' he said. 'Or perhaps I'm spying on you.'

He gave her an amused look, though something in his expression made Aliya wonder if it really had been a joke. But why would the Infinitum Council spokesperson be spying on *her*?

Neon helped her clamber over the window ledge. Once on the other side, the window swiftly turned into a wall as Neon closed the portal with his key. Nearly everything in the office was white and sleek. Also, there were circles everywhere: on Neon's shirt, on the wallpaper. The white carpet too had a circle pattern.

The sharp-edged desk, the leather sofa, it all looked sterile – a cross between a hospital and a spaceship. The only touch of colour in the room was Neon himself, whose hair had now strangely shifted from light purple to pink. He returned her stare with a smile.

'Too much white?' He gestured at the room. 'I like it. Stills the mind, you know. And I make up for it by dressing like this.' He stroked one hand over his rich golden robe, then brought it up to his head. 'What d'you think of the hair?'

Hitching up a sleeve, he showed her a futuristic-looking watch. As he touched it, a holographic screen appeared in mid-air. After some swiping and tapping, he arrived at a colour wheel. He moved the cursor on the screen and his hair began shifting colour. It went from turquoise to magenta.

'Not sure it suits me,' he said, clicking a holographic button that turned the screen into a mirror. 'Think I'll stick to the pastels.' He quickly shifted his hair back to lilac.

Aliya nodded stupidly, sitting down in the white leather-and-chrome armchair Neon offered her. 'Sherbet?' He lifted a crystal canister filled with deep-red liquid. Aliya shook her head. Back on board the *Silver Express*, Dorian, disguised as Arsinoe, had drugged her with sweetened tea, and since then she was uncomfortable taking drinks from strangers. And Neon was, after all, a stranger.

He sat down opposite her.

'You must be so upset about the locksmiths disappearing like that.'

'Yeah,' Aliya said truthfully. 'I don't believe the rumours, though.'

'It's all very distressing.' Neon shook his head. 'Which is why I'm here to help. You are the last locksmith left and the only one with access to the Smithy.'

Aliya stared at him. She had been so busy digesting the pod's spectacular failure, Geddo's illness, the locksmiths' disappearance and her own unsettling inclinations, that she had failed to realize this fact.

'OK,' she said. 'But I'm sure they'll be back soon and then—'

'I'm not sure you realize the gravity of the situation.' Neon cut in, 'Until we sort this out, I really must insist that you let me share the responsibility of keeping the Smithy safe. It's a serious task and –' he paused, steepling his fingers – 'from what I've seen, your nadim is behaving . . . erratically at present.'

'It's not what you think,' Aliya began. On her shoulder, Simi gave an affronted croak. 'We were just unlucky at the try-outs and that portal was . . .' She broke off. She couldn't tell Neon that she had somehow been involved in opening a portal to the Shop of Second Chances twice in one day . . . *if* it was her.

'That mark on her chest,' Neon said, nodding at Simi, his brow furrowed in concern. 'She needs help, and we are here for you.'

Aliya felt Simi press herself against her neck.

'The locksmiths,' she said. 'Aren't you going to search for them?'

'You're assuming they're innocent?'

'Of course they're innocent!'

Neon looked at her in silence for a moment.

'Of course,' he said at last. 'That's what the Council and I are hoping.'

Hoping? He had to be joking.

Neon went to get something from his desk. He returned with a jar, which he placed on the glass table between them. Aliya instantly recognized it. It was one of Professor Nigm's smoke jars, in which he kept his memories, shaped in smoke. She'd seen the jars arrayed on wooden shelves on the rare occasions she'd been to her mentor's home, and there would sometimes be one or two in his office at the Smithy. But she'd never noticed this one. It was black with a skull and crossbones on it, printed in red.

'I can tell you know what this is,' Neon said, looking at her intently.

She nodded. 'The smoke in them portrays Professor Nigm's memories. How did you get it?'

'Oh, we've had to search through the locksmiths' apartments . . . security protocol.'

'Search for what, exactly? And what's this?' She gestured at the smoke jar. 'Are you gonna try to convince me that my mentor's up to no good?'

'You tell me.'

Neon plucked the lid off the jar. Instantly, black smoke rose from its mouth.

It solidified in places, and thinned in others, to create a black and white image in mid-air. There was a younger Professor Nigm sitting at a desk, intently reading a thick book. Bringing out a knife, he began mumbling some inaudible incantations while pricking his finger. A drop of blood fell from the wound and, as it hit the desk, it began to grow and take shape. Aliya felt the hairs on her neck stand up. This was her mentor practising *magic*. The black shape formed into the head of what Aliya guessed was a demon, before Neon recalled the smoke by tapping the neck of the jar with its cork. It slipped back into the container, dissolving the image.

'Now, you tell me, what am I supposed to think?' Neon said.

Aliya stood up, fumbling for the armrest. Her head was swimming, her thoughts racing for some way to disprove what she had just seen, to be able to dispel it.

'This is why we need access to the Smithy,' Neon repeated. 'Why we have to insist that you hand over the responsibility.'

Standing, he took a step towards her with arms outstretched, as though he was going to embrace her. Aliya backed away, bumping into furniture. She clumsily headed for a large door, a gilded streamlined affair with circles made of glass in the pattern.

'I-I've got to go now,' she mumbled, then stopped, realizing she was being rude. 'I'm sorry,' she said, turning to face him. 'It's just . . . I can't give you access to the Smithy. It's this oath, see. We swear it when we're initiated. Only locksmiths allowed. Could you please open this door?'

Neon was looking at her with an expression she couldn't quite decipher. Was he annoyed? She couldn't tell. Facing the door, she felt her eyes prick with tears. She needed time. In front of her, the door clicked open. Neon must have used one of his remote controls.

'I understand,' he said. 'And I respect that. But before you leave, could I just give you this?'

Coming up to her, he put a piece of white metal in her hand, the shape and size of a credit card. 'It's a portal key. Run it along any doorframe and it will open into the right place. I'm throwing a small party tomorrow night. Well, it's past midnight, so tonight, rather. I would love for you to come. Perhaps we can sort out this whole debacle about the try-outs, yes? If they heard your side of the story, I'm sure they'd give you another chance.'

Aliya looked from Neon to the portal key.

'Really?'

Despite her discomfort with the situation, Aliya knew this was an opportunity she couldn't refuse.

'Tonight at nine p.m. Don't be late.' Neon pointed at a whizzcalator that stood hovering just metres away in the courtyard outside his office door. 'Huxley will take you back to the hostel. We could've used the window portal again, but I thought you might like to ride like one of the elect.' He held open the door for her and she walked out. 'Oh, and I'm sorry about your grandfather's condition.'

Aliya turned to him.

'You know about that?'

'Of course. Your grandfather is an invaluable part of our travel community.' Neon was so close to her that she could see that his pupils were deep purple, to match his hair. Was he able to adjust their colour too?

'I've put my best people on finding an antidote to cure him.' Neon nodded gravely. 'It shouldn't be long now.'

'Are they working with Matron Olfat?' Aliya asked, suddenly excited. 'With menacin?'

Neon made a dismissive gesture.

'No, we've got our own ways. Don't worry, I'll keep you updated on their progress.'

The door closed. Aliya looked down at the portal key in her hand. From the outside, Neon's building somehow resembled the card she was holding: pure white, without any details – just a big white egg of a building.

Now the man called Huxley opened the door to the whizzcalator. Aliya stepped into the glass box and took in the futuristic buildings around them – more eggs nestled in manicured greenery.

'To the hostel, miss?' Huxley asked.

Aliya nodded, then gasped as the whizzcalator rose into the air. The ground fell away and soon they were cruising above the moonlit housetops. Below them, the ultra-modern quarter spread out, all glass facades and dramatic angles. It was beautiful in a sterile way, but Aliya was glad she lived in the hustle and bustle of the Khedivial Quarter, with its cobblestone streets and imperfect yet grand buildings made of stone and wood. She shivered, suddenly feeling the chill of the night, then looked down at the white portal key in her hands. Something about Neon made her uneasy . . . he was too perfect, almost unreal. But maybe this was a way to set something right at least. If her pod could somehow get to join the Great Race, she could go look for the lost locksmiths. And if it was true that Neon could help Geddo, he had just become the most important person in her life.

Chapter 7
THE SMOKE BRACELET

'I'll do the talking once we get in front of the Council.' Victoria held up the white portal key she had snatched from Aliya the moment she had told them about the meeting. 'You've caused enough damage to the pod already. This is our last chance.'

'You don't think they're still going ahead with the race?' Mustafa gestured at the television that stood in the common room cosy corner, showing scenes from Qahira Square where crowds had gathered to protest against the locksmiths. 'So what's the point of asking for another chance to be Sweepers?'

'It's the principle.' Victoria gave a prim nod. 'I've never lost anything in my life, and I'm not starting now.'

It was morning, and the pod had gathered for breakfast in their own common room. Since the failure at the try-outs, none of them felt like mixing in the downstairs dining hall with the rest of the students, who would have an ample supply of pity or mockery in store. Aliya wasn't sure which was worse. Also, overnight, what had been a whispered resentment against the locksmiths had risen to a crescendo. When Aliya had made her way upstairs to check on Geddo after waking up, she had received several hostile looks from the students she had met on the stairs.

Aliya glanced around at her podmates as they ate. The only reason they were all gathered this morning, rather than each having their usual hurried breakfast on the go, was because of the disaster last night – classes and apprentice duties had been suspended because of the disappeared locksmiths. Despite the tension between her and Karima it felt good that they were all there, the whole pod, gathered around the table just like they used to before everyone got too busy. Since their initiation last year, the friends didn't take most classes together.

'Don't forget it was Aliya who got us the chance by meeting with Neon,' Mustafa said to Victoria, before taking a bite of his sandwich.

'The least she could do,' Victoria huffed.

Aliya, who had finished her first portion of baked pumpkin with béchamel, got up to revisit the breakfast Mrs Dickens had prepared on a wheeled cart. Aliya could tell from the food spread that she was still feeling sorry for them. Along with the usual Egyptian breakfast items there was a large trifle with layers of red jelly, custard and sponge. The wintry morning sun made the day feel fresh and bright, and as she sampled the trifle Aliya couldn't help feeling hopeful, despite Victoria's thunderous mood.

'Aliya has to use it,' Aion mumbled, looking at them from under her zebra-striped fringe. 'The invitation . . . the portal key. It'll be coded to respond to her only. It's fancy tech. Kind of thing the uber-rich use back home, you know, to make sure only the right people can get into their parties.'

Fuad took the invitation from Victoria and looked it over. 'Think you could crack this?' he asked Aion. 'Make it admit all of us?'

Fuad and Aion were forever trying to find new ways of upgrading ordinary items to have new functions. Their common room toaster now scorched messages into their evening toast, mostly dictated by Victoria (*Stake out the area! Look for portals! Report back! Regroup!*). The common room toilet played music when you opened the lid. It had two settings: electronic music that Aion claimed helped with constipation, and whale song, which helped with the runs.

'Whatever.' Victoria snatched the key back. 'Once we're in, I'm doing the talking.'

Victoria carried her plate over to join Karima, who had finished eating and was sitting in front of the TV, still showing the news. Aliya sighed. Since she had accused Karima of giving up on developing an antidote for Geddo, she hadn't said a word to her. Back in their shared room, they had avoided each other in grumpy silence. Aliya supposed Karima was waiting for her to apologize, but she was not quite ready.

Victoria cranked up the sound on the TV.

'Shh!' she hissed at Fuad and Aion, who were

discussing the key. 'They're talking about the race!'

Neon Ticker's pale face filled the screen. This morning his hair was green, as were his eyes.

'Do you really mean to say that the Great Race will go ahead as scheduled tomorrow?' a light-blue genie reporter asked him.

'That's right, Tamara,' Neon said. *'I've sent my best team to complete the course, and we've got everything in hand. There's no reason to give those who conspire against us the satisfaction of ruining such an important event.'*

'The race is going ahead?' Mustafa looked at the others in surprise.

'See?' Victoria looked around. 'We've got to talk to the Council tonight. They've *got* to make us Sweepers.'

Aliya frowned. Neon was talking as if the locksmiths' treason was a certainty. Ignoring Victoria, who had begun to rant about how to convince the Council, she focused on the genie reporter, who was now interviewing travellers at Grand Central Station.

'Do you think it is a conspiracy?' the interviewer

asked a sphinx in a turban and a green velvet cape. 'Do you believe the locksmiths are planning to take over the travel world?'

'Who knows what they were up to in that secret workshop of theirs,' the sphinx said. 'I'm not one for rumours, but one can't help wondering why they've got so many secrets. And then, to leave that little girl in charge of the most volatile place in the whole of the travel world . . . It's irresponsible, that's what!'

'Have they all gone mad? Don't they hear themselves?' Aliya turned to Mustafa, who was closest to her. 'First they're accusing the locksmiths of trying to take over the travel world, and then for leaving it behind and—'

At that moment an image appeared on the television, shocking Aliya into silence. The smoky form of Professor Nigm practising magic was expanding in the air over Qahira Square. Neon had opened the smoke jar and showed everyone her mentor's secret shame. The pod stared at the scene in silence, at the gathered crowd of onlookers who gradually got angrier and began cursing the locksmiths. Finally, Mustafa got up and switched the TV off.

All faces turned to Aliya, even Karima's. For a moment, Aliya thought she recognized that same suspicion in their faces as she had seen in the faces of the other students – the ones she had met that morning on the stairs. Stung, she got up and left.

Aliya arrived at the Ottoman Quarter out of breath and with a pounding headache. Professor Nigm lived in a faculty building connected to the Chronology Department – a beautiful two-storey house full of decorative wooden arches, painted tiles and calligraphy. Above her, beyond the housetops, the smoky image of her mentor performing magic was still playing on a loop, cutting off exactly when the blood began to turn into the figure of a demon, then starting over. It hung in the sky, an ominous backdrop to the serene quarter with its flowing fountains and shaded courtyards. To escape the view, Aliya quickly slipped into the professor's building. She had come with the intention of breaking into his flat to search for something that could explain the grotesque image, as well as some clue as to what could have happened to him and the other locksmiths.

As she walked through the marble corridor that led to the professor's flat, the ground beneath her seemed to shift, just like her conviction about her mentor. If Nigm was not what she thought he was, then were those rumours about the locksmiths true? Did they have a tendency towards the dark? The image of the Darkling slid past in her mind's eye, chilling her to the bone. If the locksmiths were thrown into question, what did that say about her?

Aliya hadn't been to the professor's home often. They usually met at the Smithy. Still, the heavy wooden door with its tulip-shaped knocker felt familiar, as if she were standing in front of a place she had visited a thousand times. In her despair, she hadn't thought of how she was going to get into the flat. Grabbing the handle, she inserted a hairpin into the lock, the way she'd seen thieves do in movies, only to jump back when a plume of smoke shot out and settled before her. Nigm stood there, or a smoke version of him did, complete with his onion turban and calm, forbidding expression. Aliya stared at the honey-coloured smoke that made up his nose. Seeing him now, looking just like she was used to and so unlike that younger self that was displayed across the Citadel sky, she wasn't sure what to feel. All those months of togetherness, of trusting him, couldn't be wiped out in a moment, could they?

'Dear visitor,' the figure began. 'You have come to find me away or unable to receive you. Please return at a later time. If you wish, I can take a message.'

'I-I need to get into your . . . I mean the professor's office,' Aliya said. 'It's really important . . . an emergency, actually. Can you let me in?'

'Hmm,' the smoky image of Nigm said. 'Before I do that, I need to ask you a question – a question only a most trusted companion would be able to answer.'

'OK,' Aliya said, her nervousness spiking. What if the professor didn't find her trustworthy? All her blunders, her foolish mistakes – what did he really think of her? Did he regret ever having made her his apprentice? 'Go ahead.'

'What is very special about a silver lantern I keep on a shelf in my sitting room?'

Aliya looked down at her shoes.

'It contains dark blue smoke,' she told the figure,

'which takes the shape of your late wife and daughter when released. They died in an earthquake.'

Nigm had shown it to her once, perhaps to comfort her over her own lost family. It was a gesture she would never forget. The tall smoke figure slipped to the side and dissolved as the heavy door clicked open. Aliya exhaled in relief, and stepped inside.

Aliya spent a good hour in Nigm's study, searching through letters, documents and papers, with no luck. Around her, Nigm's many chronological devices ticked and buzzed. When she had gone through the drawers twice, she turned to a bookcase crammed full of books, manuscripts and papers. She had reached the top shelf when two amber eyes gleamed out at her.

'Mish-Mish,' Aliya breathed. 'You scared me half to death!'

A Persian cat nimbly jumped off the shelf into an armchair. Aliya sat down on the chair she had stood on to reach. She had completely forgotten about the odd pet the professor had recently inherited from an old traveller aunt who had passed away. Mish-Mish wasn't strictly a cat, but a breed of genie that usually manifested as one. He could transform into almost any type of feline but seemed to prefer Persians.

'You can't blame me for hiding away in this dreadful city.' Mish-Mish gave her a languid look. 'Haven't you noticed the way they treat mythicals around here? I'm better off as a cat.'

Aliya nodded. According to Mustafa, whose work at the Refuge kept him updated on all things mythical, discrimination against them was worse than ever in the Citadel. The incidents usually involved accusations of magic. Those who did not want to admit that Dorian was back felt more comfortable blaming the sphinxes who guarded their buildings, or the genies and ghouls who served them at restaurants or worked in the Citadel shops. The town's unspoken rule was that mythicals were best as servants. Only very few, like Salman the half-troll, ever managed to become travellers.

'Do you know anything about what's happened?' she asked. 'About Nigm and the locksmiths? Did he say anything?'

Mish-Mish stared at her in silence for some moments. Then, stretching out a paw, he tipped over a small wooden box. As it fell to the ground its contents – a purple plume of smoke – remained hanging in the air. The smoke took the shape of another Professor Nigm.

'If you are seeing this, chances are I have disappeared,' the figure began. 'I prepared this, Aliya, knowing you would come looking for me. While I can't tell you exactly what has happened to me, I can tell you why. For months, I've been investigating the activities of a secret society of futurists known as the Loopers. I don't know their exact plans, except that they will benefit an elect few and be devastating to the rest.' The image of Nigm paused, as if deliberating what to say next. 'Please don't do anything rash, Aliya. Your talents are not yet . . . matured. Stay safe. Help *will* come to you in the shape of the Night Folk. Now, before I go, I must give you one last important message. Whatever you do, don't let *anyone* into the Smithy. Don't trust anyone who tries to get in. Use the smoke bracelet to find me.'

As the last word rang out, the figure dissolved into thin air – all except a tendril of smoke that snaked its way over to Aliya and wrapped itself around her wrist. Aliya looked down at the strange thing, effervescent and solid at once.

'The Loopers?' She looked up at Mish-Mish. 'So there is a conspiracy, after all, just not by the locksmiths, but by these . . . futurists?'

But the genie had retreated back into his hideout among the books on the top shelf.

If the Loopers were behind the locksmiths' disappearance, Aliya thought with sudden hope, *the locksmiths might not be guilty of anything*. Still, it didn't explain why Nigm had been practising magic. She would have to locate him to find out the truth.

'It won't be easy,' came Mish-Mish's voice from above. 'Finding the locksmiths. They've been taken by time-travellers with access to all of history, perhaps even the future.'

Aliya looked up at him in horror. She hadn't considered the fact that the locksmiths could be in danger, that they had been *kidnapped*. And travelling outside of one's native time was dangerous. It needed careful planning and access to chronobaric chambers. She remembered the slideshow one of her teachers had shown her class, depicting travellers who, for some reason or another, had failed to follow travel protocol. The first stage was disorientation, followed by disintegration and death.

'Maybe I should start by finding these Night Folk?' Aliya called, looking up at the spotted tail that hung down from the shelf.

'Another futile idea. You don't find the Night Folk. They find you.'

'Oh,' Aliya said. She reckoned it would be good to get help, but these Night Folk sounded frightening.

Mish-Mish's head appeared again. He had begun to transform and now looked more like an Egyptian Mau, with a grey coat and dark leopard spots.

'The professor is a kind master, which is why I'll tell you this.' He gave a wide yawn. 'That flashy human with the ever-changing hair colour . . . Last night he opened a portal through a window and came in here. Searched everywhere.'

'Neon Ticker? He was probably looking for a way into the Smithy,' Aliya said with a frown. 'What a meddler. He must have come after me when he found nothing here.' She hesitated. 'Did he take anything with him when he left . . . like one of the smoke jars?'

'I think you know that already. Don't you watch the news? Or the sky?'

Aliya's heart sank. She had hoped that the smoke image of her mentor had been fabricated somehow, perhaps through holographics. But this proved it. It was real.

That blasted Neon Ticker. What business had he displaying Nigm's guilt in front of the whole city? She would never help him, she decided, but then she remembered what he had promised about finding a cure for Geddo. She needed him, regardless of what he had done to her mentor. Still, she would never let him or anyone into the Smithy. What she had to do was find the locksmiths, and fast.

Chapter 8
THE LOOPERS

It was night. Back in the common room the pod sat gathered by the fire, looking at the portal key that lay on a table between them. The evening snack cart which Mrs Dickens had prepared stood untouched by the fireplace, a sign that something serious was afoot. Just moments earlier, Aion, who had been studying Neon's portal key, had discovered something strange.

'It leads to a trap portal,' Aion explained. 'The moment you step through it, you'll be caught in a cage. It's what the police in my time use to catch criminals.'

Aliya looked at the others in horror.

'What's Ticker up to?' she exclaimed. 'I mean,

who does that?'

She couldn't believe the lengths to which Neon was willing to go to make her give him access to the Smithy.

'The Council really means business,' Victoria said grimly. 'They might throw you in prison if you don't cooperate.'

Aliya remembered how nice Neon had been, how easy-going. He'd been odd, yes, but had seemed to understand her predicament – but he had obviously just been nice to get her to cooperate. That had been him playing good cop. She picked up the portal key and turned it over in her hands. To think that such an innocent-looking thing could lead to a cage.

'Why are they focusing on me anyway?' she said. 'They should be hunting down those futurists.'

The pod exchanged glances. She'd told them what she had heard in Nigm's study, of course, but wasn't sure they believed her. There had been a row. The others had insinuated that she'd made up the story about the Loopers to excuse the locksmiths. The day had been a mess of shouting and door slamming. But now the time had come to use Neon's invitation, and they had no choice except to cooperate.

Aliya sighed. She had no energy for another fight. Besides, the energy she did have left would be needed on this mission.

'So, what do we do?' Mustafa said. 'If you don't go, they'll surely search for you here.'

Aliya instinctively sought Karima's eyes, but her friend looked away. Up until two days ago, sorting this out together would have been so natural. Now . . . Karima was still waiting for an apology, but Aliya couldn't manage it, not as long as Geddo hovered dangerously close to death. That morning when she had checked on him, he had looked strangely grey, the skin of his face papery. Matron Olfat had shooed her away. Her grandfather was too tired to talk.

Gazing around at her friends, she steeled herself for what lay ahead. Regardless of Neon's tactics, she needed him to get her that antidote. That would require skill and something she wasn't very good at – tact. It would be especially hard to manage a civilized conversation with him if she got caught in a cage.

Half an hour later, the pod were gathered in front of the door leading to the common room balcony – the one they would use to open the portal. Despite Victoria's protests, Aliya had decided to only take Aion along to the meeting. Aion, who understood futuristic tech, would make sure they didn't get caught in the cage Neon had prepared for them, and operate the smartsuits to keep them hidden until they could ascertain that the Council wasn't going to send Aliya to prison.

'Don't forget the speech,' Victoria started up again. 'You've got the notes?'

Aliya tapped the pocket where she'd stuffed the bundle of notecards on which Victoria had composed an elaborate speech – a three-page-long explanation of how she, Aliya, was the reason for the pod's abject failure during the try-outs. The confession ended in a tearful plea for a second chance. She was to recite it before the Council at the party, preferably on her knees.

'Word for word,' Victoria pressed. 'And look *crushed.*'

'Well,' Aliya sighed, 'that won't take acting.'

'This is a diplomatic mission,' Victoria went on. 'So, for God's sake, be polite and don't let your bird peck at anyone. This is our last chance to be back in the game and if we don't—'

'I'm sure Aliya gets the picture,' Mustafa interrupted, laying a hand on Victoria's arm. 'She knows what's at stake.'

Victoria snorted.

'I'm not sure she does.'

Aliya took a deep breath and tried to focus. She would need her wits about her to carry off the slightly altered scheme she had in mind, which she hadn't told the others about. She was going to use the Smithy as a bargaining chip to get the antidote needed to save Geddo. If Neon could play dirty, she could too. She would make him think that she would comply, but then instead of opening the Smithy, she would do something better: she would find the locksmiths. The smoke bracelet would guide her to them. Once they were back, everything would be cleared up.

'The smartsuits will detect whatever environment you land in,' Fuad said, adjusting something on

Aliya's collar. 'Then camouflage you completely, from head to toe. Aion and I have been working on them like crazy. I tried one out this afternoon at Umut's Steakhouse. No one noticed a thing. Don't worry, I left money on the counter for the steaks I ate,' he told his sister, who was glaring. 'I'm not a thief.'

At that moment, the portal key began glowing. Aliya glanced up at the wall clock. It was nine p.m. The time had come for the portal to open. Simi, who thankfully had agreed to remain in her key form, was tucked safely in an inner pocket of her smartsuit.

'All right,' Aion said, picking up Dusty, the sausage-dog vacuum machine. She fired him up by pulling his lever-tail. 'Are you ready?'

Aliya nodded, then slid the portal key along the balcony doorframe. There was a pulse of brightness and the door slid open. A strong light shone in at them through the crack.

'Open it carefully,' Aion cautioned. 'The light's there to stop you seeing the trap.' She aimed Dusty, who was whirring furiously, wagging his metal tail. The moment she let him go, he skidded across the floor and through the portal. There was a great *zap*, and the light died down. In front of them, Dusty was captured in a cage of glowing bars. Beyond it, they could see a lush garden stretching out.

'Those bars will stun you if you touch them,' Aion said. They all gasped in sympathy as Dusty bounced off the cage wall, sparks flying.

'Come on,' Aliya said. 'Let's go.'

'Activate smartsuits,' Aion said into her wrist, where the control panel sat, and stepped forward. Aliya adjusted her silver goggles and zipped up the suit to her chin. Slipping after Aion, she pushed through the doorway, past the cage.

'Be careful!' Karima called, her face dim on the other side of the portal. Aliya sought her eyes, but Victoria pushed Karima out of the way.

'Stay focused!' Victoria's voice was the last thing Aliya heard before the portal shut and the doorway disappeared altogether. Looking down, she realized that she too had disappeared. The smartsuit had – chameleon-like – taken on the colours of whatever was behind her which, she discovered, was a wall made of glass. They were in an enormous glass dome.

Outside, an arid desert landscape melted into a black horizon.

'Strange venue for a Council party,' Aliya whispered.

'We're in the Wilderness,' Aion mumbled. 'I've seen photos of places like this in the books about the Infinitum's uncharted territories. The Infinitum's ever-expanding, right? Well, what you see there is the outermost limit. The dark over there is nothingness. It hasn't been created yet.'

Aliya suddenly felt dizzy. Could she really pull this off? Her plan to trick Neon into giving her the antidote – it had felt so clever just moments ago. Now she just felt impossibly out of her depth.

'How far do you think we are from the Citadel?' she asked Aion.

Aion shook her head.

'Far enough for this to exist without getting detected. You would need Council-approved shortcuts to get this far out. We're talking weeks of travelling across land, even by carpet.'

Inside the giant glass dome, huge chandeliers floated like clouds, unattached and glittering. A garden stretched out before them, full of exotic trees, bushes and plants, most of which Aliya had never seen before. There were rivulets running through the sumptuous landscape, over which white bridges stretched. In the distance she could see perfectly round, pod-like houses, nestled like fruits among the vegetation.

'These are not real plants.' Aion turned a leaf over to show her. Up close it was clearly artificial and run through by something that looked like thin wiring. 'It's PLAISTIC – plastic with artificial intelligence built in. Be careful what you say. Don't talk above a whisper.'

Aliya moved away from the vine-like plant she had been inspecting.

'You mean they could spy on us?' she mouthed.

Aion nodded with a disgusted frown. 'And respond to commands from whoever they're spying *for*.'

What was this? Aliya knew that the Council liked to butt into people's affairs – that was sort of their job. But plants that spied on people? This was really taking things too far.

'None of this is real. Those are most probably

cameras.' Aion pointed up at the sweeping chandeliers. 'The water too . . . probably LIQAID – smart water. Don't drink it. Once inside your body, it would know everything about you in seconds. Nanoparticles.'

'Is everything here made of some kind of smart material?' Aliya asked, freezing as one of the chandeliers swept by close above her head.

'That's the future for you,' Aion said bitterly. 'Although I've never seen anything this extreme. But don't worry. This stuff won't be able to detect our smartsuits.'

A familiar voice rang out. Aliya spun round, looking for the speaker, then realized the voice was coming from the plants and trees around them, from the ground and the water. The smart plastic apparently also worked to amplify sound. Neon Ticker's voice seeped through the artificial landscape. The eeriness raised the hairs on Aliya's neck.

'It's coming from over there,' Aion said, pointing towards a perfectly round building in the distance. Giving each other a resolute nod, the girls set off towards it.

*

The building, when they reached it, was unlocked. Slipping inside, the girls discovered a vast hall filled with people in white cloaks with hoods raised to cover their faces. The streamlined white space reminded Aliya of Neon's office. Genies moved through the crowd, carrying silver trays of drinks. Aliya and Aion edged along the curved wall, their smartsuits taking on its colour so that nothing, not even their eyes behind their smartgoggles, was visible.

Ahead of them, on a circular platform, Aliya could see Neon Ticker, dressed in a white cloak that sparkled as he moved. His hair, this evening, was light blue. A sleek microphone floated in the air in front of his face, following him.

'Dearly beloved, elect few . . .' He paused and looked out over the audience. 'It is time we proceeded with our vital business. I asked you to meet here tonight to tell you that the time draws near! Dear elect, we are creating a world where old age, sickness and disease have no place, where they will fade away into memory and be forgotten. As you know, whomever reaches the ripe age of forty will loop back and begin life once more. He or she will relive his or her life again, over and over, for eternity.' He paused again, steepling his hands as though he were about to pray. 'This is our dream, our vision. But I must again ask you to stay vigilant and committed. One false link and the chain might break. Who here wants to live unfettered by the stink and rot of *natural law*?' He said the last two words as though they were a preposterous idea. A disgusting concept.

Aliya and Aion exchanged a quick glance. What was this madness? This sure was no Council meeting.

'*Who*,' Neon hollered, 'wants to rise above nature and live like gods?!'

'Loop, loop, loop,' the crowd chanted, their voices rising, some punching the air with their fists in time to the chant. '*Loop, loop, loop.*'

They were interrupted by a low rumble. Aliya felt herself sliding into Aion.

'Earthquake,' she breathed.

Before they had a chance to move, a crack split the air right above the heads of the cloaked audience. A fearful gasp went through the crowd. Inside the rift was pure darkness. Aliya gripped Aion's hand for comfort. She'd seen rifts before, even worked on healing them, but witnessing one crack open like this was a new level of horrible. When the ground steadied once more, Neon spread his arms in a calming gesture, his cloak spreading like butterfly wings.

'No need for alarm.'

He sounded like he always did on the news, when he was glossing over Dorian's attacks as nothing to be concerned about.

'This –' he pointed at the rift – 'proves my point as to why we need to move fast. The Baraka we're siphoning off from the Citadel will only get us so far in creating our new world. We need to access the Smithy as soon as possible. Only then will we have a power supply strong enough to build the Loop. Thankfully, we've got the matter in hand. It won't be long now.'

'So that's what's causing the new disturbances,' she whispered to Aion. 'They blamed it on the locksmiths, but it's *them*. These are the futurists I told you about! The Loopers! They are siphoning energy from the Citadel to build their crazy . . . thing.'

'Our mission comes with some danger, my friends,' Neon continued. 'But think of the prize. Once the Loop is complete, we'll leave all our troubles behind us.'

'I must bring my mythical servants,' a lady called out.

'Of course, Horatia.' Neon approached the edge of the stage to address an elderly lady whose hood had slipped back to reveal her silver hair. 'The right type of mythical will be allowed to come along to serve. I do not expect you to scrub your own floors.'

There was laughter.

'How do we know they're the right type?' another person called.

'Ah.' Neon wagged a finger in the air. 'That's the question, isn't it? You there!' Neon waved at a genie who was passing below him with a tray. 'Come up here, if you please.'

The audience parted to let the genie pass, watching as he shuffled up the steps of the stage and into the spotlight. He was frail, almost bent double. Neon took the tray from him and put it on the ground.

'Stretch out your hands, slave, and let them see.'

Grudgingly, the old genie hitched up his shirt to the elbows, exposing two glowing bands around his wrists.

'Metaphysical bonds,' Aliya whispered to Aion. 'They're magic. They'll turn him to dust if he revolts.'

Aliya had seen the likes of them before. Cleo, the siren Dorian had forced to do his bidding on board the *Silver Express*, had worn one.

'That's all fine,' a greying older man called out. 'But when will the real magic be secured to complete our project?' As he turned, Aliya recognized him. He was a Council member from the Roman Quarter. This was getting worse and worse.

'I also called you here today to introduce you to the originator of our project,' Neon said. Stepping aside, he gestured to the back of the stage. A young man in flowing white robes approached. His blonde hair was combed back and fell to just below his ears. With his milky-white skin and bright blue eyes, he looked like a fairy-tale prince.

Aliya froze. For a moment the world blurred. Her

knees gave way and if not for Aion propping her up, she would have slid to the ground. It was *Dorian Darke* who stood there, as young as he had been in the photo she had seen on display at an exhibition of crimes at the Chronology Department, back in their first year. But he had to be at least a hundred years old. Not just that, he had been ravaged by magic and turned into a shadow – a sort of demon – so how could he be here, well, and *young*?

'That's him, isn't it?' Aion whispered.

Aliya nodded. 'That's my worst nightmare coming true, right there.'

'Is that you, Dorian Darke?' the Council member called out. 'We thought you were dead.'

'Death is such a flexible concept when you have time travel and magic at your disposal,' Dorian said with a faint smile. 'When Neon and I came together, we discovered the wonder of combining technology with magic. And the evidence is right here.' He gestured at himself. 'Just look at me! Am I not beautiful?'

'The marriage of magic and technology,' Neon said. 'The body Dorian is possessing is of my own design. Those of you who need new bodies will be provided with them, of course.' He looked at the old Council member. 'We only want the best, young, upgraded versions of yourselves to live for ever in the Loop.'

'It's an artificial body.' Aion shook her head in disbelief. 'And Dorian is possessing it.'

'By marrying the magic of the Shop of Second Chances with Neon's technology, we'll build a new world.' Dorian's white teeth glistened in the spotlight. 'A utopia where we'll live for ever with our loved ones, risen from beyond to join us in our bliss.'

'And when we reach the limit we've set for ourselves,' Neon continued, laying a hand on Dorian's shoulder, 'the Loop will bring us back to where we began and we'll live our lives over again, over and over, for ever. The choice morsel of existence savoured infinitely.'

'What will become of the existing travel world?' someone in the audience asked.

'It will be replaced,' Neon said simply.

'And the people in it? And mythicals?'

'When the Loop is erected, all that does not fit in

our brave new world will be . . . done away with, erased. As you all know, we simply cannot have outsiders living on that don't see the light. We really have no choice. If we spared them, they would never cease trying to destroy us and what we've built. We must be cruel to be kind.'

'Loop, loop, loop,' the crowd began chanting again. The sound of their voices echoed around the hall, low and ominous, like a heartbeat.

'Now, we've got a real treat for you,' Neon called out, and the crowd quieted. 'But we'll need a volunteer. *You.*'

Neon pointed at a ghoul waiter who stood refilling glasses amid the audience.

'Give this good mythical a round of applause,' Neon said when the ghoul, who'd been pushed and shoved through the crowd, had reached the stage.

'Please, sir,' said the ghoul, looking alarmed, his beady eyes darting for a way to escape. But he too, Aliya realized, was caught in the bonds they had seen earlier. These mythicals were all enslaved.

Dorian pulled something out of his pocket – a thing that made Aliya's blood freeze. It was his nadim: a key in the shape of a snake, biting its own tail. The Darkling.

It grew, slowly at first, then faster and faster, transforming from a metal object into a living thing – a black beast, as big as a car.

'I made my Darkling out of an *ouroboros*,' Dorian said. 'A tool the ancients used to transform magic into Baraka. But I discovered that this object can also do the exact *reverse* of what it was made for. It can suck up good energy to *feed* magic.'

He absently stroked the snake along its scales. At once, the key began to transform into a living creature.

'My Darkling has not fed for a long time. You can tell by her shrunken size. But now, go ahead, my dearest. Feed.'

The snake-nadim shot forward and coiled itself around the ghoul. Aliya watched in horror as it squeezed, the ghoul's panicked shouts becoming more and more choked until he finally collapsed. From his half-open mouth, the Darkling sucked the same glowing substance that Aliya had seen Cleo, the siren, pull out of her victims' mouths aboard the

Silver Express. The Darkling was harvesting a soul, sucking it out, then gobbling it down.

Uncoiling and dropping the ghoul's body like rubbish, the snake grew even bigger. Dorian too was changing. He suddenly lit up from inside – his artificial body beaming. Streams of light radiated from his hands. They reached the ceiling, bathing it in a luminous glow that spread along the walls, cascading down to the ground. The hall began to change. Aliya felt herself floating, her vision blinded. When she could see again, they were standing in what resembled a storybook castle. Marble pillars ran the length of the great hall. Long tables full of cream cakes, pastries and fruits had appeared. Crystal decanters of bright liquids with glasses to match appeared floating in mid-air.

'Such a noble sacrifice,' Neon yelled, 'to feed the magic! And see what it built us!'

Aliya stared at the motionless body of the ghoul on the stage, her throat tight with horror. These people were using mythicals as fodder, as something dispensable. Now, one of the audience rushed up on stage and knelt before Dorian, clutching his hand.

The magician put a glowing hand on his head. A moment later his bald scalp began sprouting hair – long, dark and glistening, like a horse's tail.

'A miracle!' Neon shouted from his place next to the magician. 'A true miracle!'

More people lined up to get their magical gifts, one losing the crutches she was using to walk, another getting taller, a third becoming thin as a wisp. The Darkling had retreated to the back of the stage, and lay coiled and quiet, satiated.

Aliya and Aion hadn't moved from their spot against the wall, even as their surroundings metamorphosed. The very air around them vibrated with magic. Aliya felt it sucking at her, making her smart-suit crackle.

'We've got to get out of here,' she told Aion, frantically stroking Simi, who had begun to transform inside her suit. 'The magic is making Simi crazy.'

'These suits aren't magic-proof,' Aion said. 'I honestly don't know what will happen if we stay here.'

At that moment, the Darkling uncoiled again. Raising itself, it sniffed the air, its forked tongue flicking out. Aliya tried to hold the suit shut, but now Simi's head was out. A second later, she had slid through the opening at Aliya's chest and was flying towards the stage, her orange crest raised.

'*Nooo!*' Aliya's horrified scream was followed by a stunned silence. Everyone turned towards the source of the sound. Simi had just about reached the Darkling when a ghoul waiter held up a silver tray and stopped her – *smack* – in mid-flight.

'Simi!' Aliya breathed.

'A distraction!' Aion cried. 'We need a distraction!'

Poof! Just as a gang of Loopers was heading for them, another ghoul waiter uncorked a carafe, releasing a weather-beaten genie who rose into the air like a gigantic dirty sheet. Seconds later, he had transformed into an enormous swarm of angry bees that spread among the Loopers, buzzing angrily.

'My nadim,' Aliya cried, desperately looking around. 'She's—'

'She's right here,' a gruff voice said next to her. 'Now come along, before something worse happens.'

Turning, Aliya looked into the face of the ghoul waiter who had stopped Simi. Before she could resist, she was picked up by the scruff of her smartsuit.

'You too!' the ghoul growled at Aion. 'Try and deploy any of your gadgets and I'll debone you like smoked mackerel. This is an order by authority of the Night Folk.'

Dazed, Aliya watched the ghoul use his free hand to fish out an ordinary-looking zipper – the kind you would sew into the fly of a pair of trousers. Hanging it in thin air, he unzipped it. A dark pocket of space opened.

'In you go,' he urged. 'And be quick about it. Don't mind the drop. Try to fall bum first to avoid getting knocked on the head.'

Moments later, Aliya was falling through darkness with Simi in her arms, screaming at the top of her lungs.

Chapter 9
THE GRIZZLED HEN

Aliya woke to the sound of faraway voices. There were four of them, she counted dazedly, and they sounded like old toads croaking.

She opened her eyes. Looking down at her was a small wooden face with a long twig nose that ended in a cluster of blackish berries.

Sitting up, she discovered that she was in a strange bed and that the long-nosed face belonged to a bedpost guardian. There were three more of them, equally twig-nosed. Seeing her awake stirred the guardians into a higher pitch, and from the snippets Aliya managed to understand, they were asking questions about her and answering them themselves. Aliya rolled her eyes, despite her alarm.

Bedpost guardians weren't exactly the most rational beings. Perhaps this was because they, like all such mythical artefacts, had been blotted of magic upon entry into the travel world.

'Where am I?' she asked, her voice barely audible. She looked around for Aion. 'Where's my friend?'

The guardians stared back at her.

'Where am I?' she heard one of them mimicking. 'Well, I'm here, of course.'

'We're here, of course,' said another. 'Where else would we be?'

Aliya fought with the tweed blanket that ensnared her legs. There were drapes around the four-poster, also tweed, which prevented her from seeing the rest of the room.

In a rush, the events leading up to her present condition came back to her: the Loopers' meeting in the Wilderness, being saved by a ghoul, Aion and Simi . . . Oh, Simi. Aliya fumbled in the half-light, looking for the nadim. She found her sleeping on a pillow at the opposite corner of the bed. She recalled Simi flapping her way over the heads of the congregated Loopers to reach the Darkling. Looking down at the slumbering bird, she had the urge to slap her awake, or shake her . . . choke her. What was she doing? With a sickening lurch, Aliya remembered that she too had felt drawn to the Darkling when they had been close at the try-outs. The thought was still raw in her mind. What was happening to them?

And the Loopers . . . It was absolutely mad, wasn't it, to build a perfect world through magic? But it was a world where one could escape from sickness, old age and death. When Neon had said he could get her an antidote for Geddo, had he meant a magic one? Since Geddo's stab wound had been caused by magic, it might need a magic remedy to heal . . .

The smartsuit that she was still wearing felt tight and uncomfortably hot against her skin. Picking up Simi, she peeked out of the curtains. The room around her was neat and smelt faintly of boiled broccoli. A single armchair, also upholstered in a tweed material, stood by the fireplace. With a jolt she realized who this place must belong to. She only knew one person who liked tweed this much!

'Mr Kamel!' she called out. When no one answered, she got out of bed and crossed to the door.

Pushing through into the room beyond, she ran smack into a broad back. The figure that turned to peer down at her was not her grandfather's butler, but the scariest-looking sphinx she had ever seen. His black, greasy hair hung down the sides of his furrowed face all the way to his muscular cat torso. Fangs hung from his upper lip like two rusted daggers. They matched the giant claws of his front paws. Aliya winced as the beast swung his tail. A long blade was attached to its end – the only thing about the figure that looked polished.

The parlour before her was crowded with characters who looked like they had come out of a handbook on how to look scary. Most of them were sitting around a long wooden table having breakfast. A steaming samovar stood at the centre, surrounded by chunky loaves, and an assortment of sausages, jams, honey, eshta, zaatar and cheeses.

At the far end, a tall mythical whom Aliya suspected was a sila sat enveloped in a billowing cape that she realized was an actual thundercloud – a cloud she seemed to be keeping in check by stroking it calmingly. Just like the silas Aliya had previously met, this mythical's personality was merged with weather. Her embrace was full of rumbling thunder and cracks of lightning that lit up her gaunt face. Part of the cloud had escaped her and was drizzling into a pot of fuul. Next to her sat a fierce-looking ghoul in furs, gobbling two sausages at a time. Then came a couple of creatures Aliya had only read about, but never seen. There was a baebue, a large man-like creature with claws instead of nails, and no pupils in his eyes. Aliya watched in horror as he ate, using his claws to spear the sausages.

By the fireplace, Aliya spotted Aion caught in the lap of a massive ghoul lady. The ghoul was feeding her friend green porridge with a spoon so big it only just fitted in her mouth. Spotting Aliya, her friend shot her a pleading look.

'So, you're awake at last,' a familiar voice said. Mr Kamel appeared carrying a frying pan where one giant egg sizzled. Aliya exhaled in relief.

'You're cooking?' she asked. Kamel was wearing a sunflower-patterned apron which Aliya guessed must have been a gift from Mrs Dickens. She had never seen the genie butler eat anything, let alone cook.

'Well, none of these oafs would lend a hand,' Mr Kamel said. 'And they had to be fed. I would hate to see them turn you and your friend into their breakfast. Roc egg?'

He nodded at the frying pan. Aliya shook her head.

'How are you doing over there, Magda?' Kamel called out to the ghoul who was feeding Aion.

'This maggot pudding will fatten her up in no time,' Magda muttered. 'Just in time for the barbecue on Friday.'

At this, Aion spat out the green goo in her mouth. Letting her go, Magda burst into roaring laughter, which the rest of the room joined her in. Even Mr Kamel, who never laughed, smiled wryly.

'Let me introduce you to the Night Folk,' he said when the raucous laughter had died down. 'This is an army I've been putting together, composed of mythicals like myself. As you saw at the Loopers' meeting, the plan is to turn our kind into slaves, if we're allowed to live at all.'

'What is this place?' Aliya asked, edging away from the door and the hulking sphinx with the black hair, towards Mr Kamel, her beacon of safety in this rough crowd.

'This is the Grizzled Hen, a guesthouse on the outskirts of the Citadel,' Kamel said. 'It's where I stay when I'm here. Or did you imagine I live in a lantern?'

Aliya shook her head, then glanced around with new interest. She *had* thought Mr Kamel lived in a lantern, but wasn't going to admit that now.

'That's your bedroom in there, right?' Aliya pointed back the way she had come. 'And your bedpost guardians?'

'I enjoy listening to their bickering,' Mr Kamel said. 'Reminds me of my sisters. The snooze berries on their noses are a great remedy for insomnia.' He tapped the side of his nose.

Yuck, Aliya thought. She'd never eat something that had fallen off someone's nose, even if that nose was a twig.

She took the rest of the room in. It had yellow curtains, large bunches of dried flowers hanging from the ceiling and colourful rag rugs on the floor. The air smelt of vanilla, cooking grease and unwashed fur.

'This is Madame Magda's place.' He indicated the ghoul by the fire. 'The Grizzled Hen is a guesthouse for mythicals. It's also the headquarters of the Night Folk. Well, the cellar is. Top-secret lair under here, you see.' He pointed at a cupboard in a corner. 'Only opens to the right number of knocks, stomps and roars.'

'Nigm told us about you,' Aliya said, looking around at the assembly. 'Does Geddo know?'

Mr Kamel lit his pipe and exhaled a thin, green stream of smoke. It smelt of boiled broccoli. Mr Kamel's outlandish tobacco had once disgusted her. Now it filled her with sudden nostalgia.

'He knows we exist, but not much more. I did not want to burden him.'

'What about the Brigade? Are you working with them?'

A hum went through the crowd.

'The Brigade are out of touch, and long past their best,' the sila with the thundercloud said. 'But they refuse to admit it. We can't wait for them to save us.'

'It's our kind the Loopers are targeting,' said the sphinx with the greasy hair. 'Their sayyads – trappers

– have captured a good few of us already... sneaking into the Refuge, pretending to be from the Reform and Civilization programme.'

Aliya remembered Mustafa telling her about disappearances from his workplace. So *this* was the reason.

'We saw enslaved mythicals at the meeting,' she said, remembering the waiters with their glowing armbands, the metaphysical bonds that kept them trapped.

Kamel pulled out a chair at the table and invited Aliya to sit.

'I'm afraid you're once again at the centre of the storm,' he said.

'I know,' Aliya said. 'They're gonna try to make me open the Smithy so they can use the Sublimes' power to make their magic invincible.'

'That's the gist, yes,' Kamel said.

'But I'll never let them in.' Aliya frowned. 'I don't care what they do to me.'

At the end of the table, the thundercloud sila gave her an approving nod.

'Their conspiracy runs deep. That's why we can't

face them head on,' Kamel said. 'This mission requires cleverness, not brawn.'

'Well, then, you're out of luck with this crowd,' Madame Magda said. There was some laughter.

'We need to find the locksmiths as soon as possible,' Kamel said. 'Without them the Smithy is in terrible peril. Let's just hope they're still alive.'

'If they've been kept in a non-native time, they've only got so long.'

It was a siren with long purple hair who had spoken, her words pulling at Aliya's heartstrings, the way the voice of her kind always did. Aliya remembered Cleo, the siren she had met on the *Silver Express*, who had twice nearly pulled her soul out of her body.

'How long?' Aliya asked, keeping her eyes on the floor, safe from the siren's magnetic gaze.

'Three days at most. They will suffer disorientation at first, then sink into a coma. That's the last stage before disintegration and death.'

Aliya remembered the chronobaric chamber she had visited during her holiday stay at Karima and Fuad's in the 1930s, to avoid those ill effects. They were a fundamental part of time-travel life. 'Of course, they have to be in some time other than their own,' she said. 'They're *all* from different ages. And three days . . . that's hardly any time at all!'

'And one of those days has already passed,' said Kamel. 'Which is why some of us will travel through the racecourse they've created to search for any trace of them.' He gestured at the assembled Night Folk. 'This here crowd have senses as sharp as the most talented police dog.'

'What about us?' Aliya asked, exchanging a look with Aion. 'You're not going to tell us that it's too dangerous and that we should stay home?'

'I wouldn't if it was up to me.' Kamel regarded her. 'As I've told you before, it's no wonder most humans are so soft and useless – your parents coddle you something terrible. But you're not my child. I have been entrusted to keep you safe by your grandfather, which is why you do indeed need to stay here with Magda at the Grizzled Hen.'

'But this is our fight too!' Aliya protested, feeling her ears grow hot. 'Are you going to leave us here to rot?'

'There are plenty of rotten things around here without you making an addition.' Mr Kamel glanced at one of the ghouls' beards, which did look suspiciously green. 'Don't worry, Magda will keep you busy. She's got a herd of ostriches out back that need feeding and grooming . . . for instance.'

'Ostriches?' Aliya said in disgust. 'Are you joking? But how will you even join the race? Will you be allowed?'

'Undercover,' the thundercloud sila said. 'We'll take the place of the maintenance team.'

'And what about the real one?' Aliya asked. 'Have you asked to replace them?'

There was an awkward silence.

'They've come down with the flu,' Kamel said. 'Very unfortunate.'

'Something they ate,' said the ghoul with the rotten beard. The genie next to him jabbed him in the ribs.

'Oh, I see,' Aliya said, narrowing her eyes at Kamel. 'They'll be *all right*, I hope?'

'Perfectly,' Mr Kamel said.

Aliya and Aion exchanged another look. It was

not the first time she'd suspected that Mr Kamel had used techniques that weren't exactly Infinitum-approved. But this was a crisis, so she guessed they'd have to flex the rules a little, as long as no one got hurt.

And that, she thought as she sipped the tea Kamel had poured her, *is exactly what Aion and I will do too, to get out of this house arrest.*

'I think he would be disappointed if we didn't at least try to escape,' Aliya said to Aion later, when they had been put to work by Madame Magda, caring for her menagerie of animals. She really did have ostriches.

It was late morning and Mr Kamel and a group of Night Folk had left to start their search for the locksmiths. Stepping out into the crisp morning, Aliya and Aion had discovered that the rustic guesthouse lay in an oasis surrounded by a sea of sand. The Grizzled Hen sat snug among groves of date palms with silvery crowns that rustled high above them in the breeze.

Apart from the ostriches, there were a bunch of

quarrelsome goats that had chased Aliya around their enclosure when she tried to feed them.

'But how do we escape from here?' Aion gestured at the desert landscape around them. 'We're still quite far from the Citadel. Don't tell me we're going to ride ostriches.'

Aliya plucked Simi out of a bucket of bird feed.

'There's nothing for it. I've got to open a portal.'

The girls had discovered that the mythicals used a portal to get to and from town, located in a kitchen pantry. With much disappointment, they had also found that it couldn't be opened with a travel key, or even with the help of Simi.

'Oh, that won't open without the secret password,' Madame Magda informed them when she caught them attempting an escape. 'Followed by the right sequence of knocks and grunts.'

Kamel had taken extra precautions to keep them stranded.

When they'd finished feeding the animals and had ascertained that Magda was busy in the kitchen, the girls sneaked away and found a ramshackle log store hidden from view by the ostrich enclosure. At the sight of the shed, Simi, who was sitting on Aliya's shoulder, croaked and raised her crest. Escaping out of rooms Mr Kamel had locked her in as a form of house arrest had been a recurring challenge during the year the genie butler had spent living with her and Geddo back in Cairo. Now, being a locksmith with a nadim, she'd stepped up her game. A stupid pantry-portal wasn't going to keep her from where she wanted to go.

'She approves,' Aliya said, surprised, lifting the nadim down and stroking her over the crest – the command for her to switch to key mode. 'Let's be quick, before she changes her mind.'

This time the nadim had, for her own elusive reasons, decided to cooperate. Perhaps she sensed the urgency of Aliya continuing her quest to find the locksmiths. Perhaps she had her own reasons for getting them out of there. There was no way of telling. In time, with the blackness that was spreading across her feathers, Simi was slipping away from Aliya, becoming more of an enigma with each passing day.

Standing before the crooked door that was to

become their portal, Aliya broke out in a cold sweat. What if they ended up at the Shop again? With Simi possibly turning towards magic, would she accept closing the portal if that was what happened?

A lump in her throat, Aliya closed her eyes and thought of their common room at the hostel. She recalled the worn sofas, the maroon curtains. Somewhere familiar. Somewhere safe . . . The energy pulsed from her hand through the key and into the lock.

'Yes!'

Aion had pulled the door open, and there, on the other side of the doorway, their bewildered podmates were staring back at them from their breakfast table.

An hour later, after several cups of hot chocolate, Aion and Aliya had told the others about everything that had happened, about Neon, Dorian, the Loopers. Their podmates were all pale with shock, even though Aliya got the feeling that Victoria mostly was disappointed about not getting to plead their case to the Council.

'Neon Ticker?' Mustafa shook his head. 'But he's on the Council.'

'So, it wasn't the locksmiths at all,' Karima said, looking at Aliya fully for the first time since their quarrel. 'They are innocent.'

'Don't sound so surprised,' Aliya snapped. She hadn't forgotten that her podmates had suspected them and, by extension, *her*. And then there was that other thing . . . Karima giving up on Geddo's antidote. She hadn't forgotten that either. Although now, feeling the way she did, equal parts exhausted and afraid, she suddenly wished for nothing more than them going back to the way they'd used to be.

She must have given Karima a weird look because she frowned and said, 'What? I'm just relieved, that's all.'

'Yeah,' Aion said. 'That smoke image of Professor Nigm doing magic must've been some kind of hologram. Never seen one look like that before. I mean, it really did look like smoke. But then Neon's ahead of me on the timeline. He's got tech my time is just beginning to develop.'

Aliya nodded, even though she didn't share the others' relief about the locksmiths. Because what she knew, and they didn't, was that the smoke jar had been real. It was not a hologram, or any other kind of illusion. Her mentor really had captured a memory in smoke of himself doing magic, and he had kept it in a jar in his home. A jar that she knew had gone missing. Had the others been right in suspecting the locksmiths?

They spent the rest of the day planning a way to sneak on to the course of the Great Race to search for the locksmiths. They had to be the ones to search for them, because they had something the Night Folk didn't — the smoke bracelet Professor Nigm had left for Aliya to find him. Once found, the locksmiths would protect the Smithy from the Loopers, just like she had planned. Still, once or twice during their planning, as the danger of their mission became clear to her, Aliya almost regretted not showing the smoke bracelet to Mr Kamel. Maybe if he had seen it, he would have taken her along with the Night Folk and not insisted on leaving her behind at Madame Magda's. But then there was no way of telling what he would have done. Besides, Nigm had given *her* the task of finding him. And, she thought bitterly, she didn't want a bunch of strangers around when she faced her mentor with his criminal past.

After much discussion, the pod decided to disguise themselves and take the place of the Nepos, who were sweeping for the Ghoulies. The only question now was how to prevent the other pod from showing up.

'I just made a new batch of macaroons,' Karima offered. 'You know, the ones I make for Papa's insomnia. They don't even turn your hair pink any more! I could send them to the Nepos' common room tonight. They'll think it's a treat from Mrs Dickens and gobble them. It will make them sleep in and miss the race tomorrow. They'll be impossible to wake. You could shoot a cannon next to them and they wouldn't bat an eye.'

'Are you sure that's not mean?' Mustafa asked.

'Knowing what we know, we're doing them a favour by keeping them home,' Victoria said. But she did look a bit pleased at the prospect of pranking the Nepos, even if it was out of necessity, and ultimately for their benefit. Keeping them asleep was keeping them safely away from the race and the Loopers' plans.

Throughout the evening, the preparations continued. To avoid detection by the Night Folk, who by now must have discovered the children's escape from the Grizzled Hen, they hid out in the dark, spiderweb-festooned attic, just above Geddo's rooms. To make sure Mr Kamel or anyone else wouldn't find them, Fuad attached a fake cobweb complete with a large, dried spider over the trapdoor entrance, making it look as though no one had opened it in ages.

When night came, Karima went off to deliver her macaroons, using a smartsuit to disguise herself as one of the ghoul maids. They spent the rest of the evening preparing for the race by helping Aion sort out kinks in their suits. With them set to display the grey overalls with the matching caps and goggles that all Sweepers wore for the race, the pod would hopefully pass for the Nepos.

Just before midnight, when the hostel was quiet,

Fuad and Victoria climbed down the stairs and made their way into the night through the kitchen door, avoiding the sphinxes who slept outside the main entrance. They returned an hour later with a battered Persian rug they had selected from Professor Kashmir's carpet stable. The professor had not asked any questions when Victoria claimed her father needed a carpet from which to supervise the next day's event at Qahira Square. Playing the daddy card had paid off for once.

Finally, when all was ready, the pod sank into a fretful slumber. All but Aliya, who made her way down the attic stairs to stand outside her grandfather's door. She didn't dare knock – he would be asleep.

Don't worry, she wrote on a slip of paper she'd torn from Karima's menacin prescription pad. *I've gone to find you an antidote. Will be back soon. Hang in there, please.*

She stuck the note under the door, then lingered for a moment. She would have loved to check on Geddo, just to make sure he was all right, but she couldn't afford the risk. He might have heard the news from Mr Kamel about their escape from the Grizzled Hen. She leant her brow against the cool wood of the door and sighed. Her quest for the antidote had become fraught. Not only was the person who might help her get it a dangerous criminal, but the cure itself was probably magic. Still, she had no choice but to somehow convince Neon to give it to her. Magic or not, she needed it. That meant catching up with the very person who was chasing *them*. But how would she get the leader of the Loopers to give her what she wanted without fulfilling *his* plans?

Chapter 10
THE RACE BEGINS

Aliya took a deep breath, trying to calm her hammering heart. She ran her hand over the fringe of the large, hovering carpet, and felt it twitching under her. Whether this was a sign of anxiety or excitement she did not know, but she suspected that Marauder, the race carpet, was taking all the hullabaloo better than her.

Below them, Qahira Square was packed. There was a strange tension in the air. From the windows, balconies and even the rooftops of the department buildings more travellers stood watching, but the festive cheer that usually accompanied events like this was missing. The previous day, the pod had brought a radio with them to their hideaway in the attic and Aliya had followed the upheaval that still raged in the city – some of it caused by the locksmiths' disappearance and supposed treason, and some by the fact that the Great Race was going ahead as if nothing had happened.

The only thing bright and sure that morning was the winter sun, which rose over the competitors already seated on their carpets, waiting for the signal that would set the Great Race in motion. Aliya drew a hand over Marauder's velvety red pattern, finding a mended tear that ran like a scar through the fibre. *Not easily spooked*, Marauder's tag had read, along with comments like, *fast and steady flyer*, and *enjoys a proper brush after a long day of flying*. The carpet had a five-star rating on Quickflies, the Infinitum review app for flying vehicles.

Behind her to the right sat Victoria, her blonde hair styled to resemble that of Francesca Flux's, the Nepos' navigator. She was looking equal parts panicked and determined, her navigator kit tucked safely into the satchel she wore slung crosswise around her chest. To make the pod pass for the Nepos, Aion and Fuad had set their smartsuits to resemble the other Sweepers' outfits: grey overalls with matching goggles. Aliya looked down at the bracelet of smoke. It was the colour of thunderclouds and had not indicated anything since it had settled itself around her wrist in Nigm's office. Would it really help her find the locksmiths?

Turning, Aliya gave Mustafa, who looked carpet-sick already, a sympathetic nod, then glanced at Karima, who sat at the very back next to her menacin supply, disguised as a carpet-maintenance kit. Next to her, Aion and Fuad were hunched in concentration over the complicated remote that controlled the pod's smartsuits. Just as they'd planned, the Nepos had not appeared that morning. Aliya imagined them waking up late that afternoon to discover that they had missed the whole day and the race. They would be furious, of course, but they would understand later – at least, she hoped so. This race was no longer about skill and glory – it was a rescue mission.

She adjusted the knowledge turban Fuad had 'borrowed' from the Stealth Department to help them navigate the times they would pass through –

an upgraded version of the general-knowledge turbans for sale at most Citadel equipment stores. Glancing upwards, she could see the tip of the golden cannon that would fire the starting shot. At the very centre of the square was the first portal – a wooden cupboard, ordinary in every way, except it wasn't. The moment the cannon went off and the portal opened, they would soar through to another time and place. Once they landed in that mystery location, they would have to navigate to the next portal which, according to the rules, could be as far as a couple of kilometres away, to follow in the locksmiths' wake. That was unless the smoke bracelet led them elsewhere.

A half-hearted cheer went through the crowd as a group of hieracosphinxes appeared, flexing their wings rhythmically. Bombastic music poured out over the square and the hieracos began the dance Aliya had seen them practising in the Smithy. Next to her, Mustafa tensed. Apparently, his issue with the sphinxes still hadn't been resolved.

She felt Simi flap her wings on her shoulder, invisible after a rub with an invisibility cream. It had been a relief to make the nadim disappear, if only for a short while. Every time Aliya caught sight of the ever-growing black patch on her chest, difficult questions surged inside her – questions she had no answers to.

In front of her, hovering at slightly different heights, were the competing pods on their carpets. Despite the Council's guidance for pods to keep a low profile, the Janissaries from Mehmet Nazim's Hostel wore glittering chainmail and golden helmets, and were looking as fierce as ever. The pod from Hippolyta's Hostel in the Ptolemaic Quarter, the Philosophers, looked less savage in pink, but fitted for speed on board a silvery carpet.

Aliya searched the crowd, looking for Loopers. They would be here, of course, somewhere – probably searching for *her*. The thought sent a cold shiver up her spine. Mr Kamel and the Night Folk were probably on the lookout for her as well. The butler was no doubt hidden in the square somewhere, waiting to enter the course. That meant she couldn't remove the smart face shield she was wearing, for even a second. The shield was made of thin, breathable material but still – the sensation of something stuck to her face was hard to ignore.

A commotion just in front of them snapped her to attention. The Ghoulies, with Salman Bashiri at the helm, were vying for the best spot in front of the door by shoving the Philosophers and their carpet to the side. Aliya could see Salman's beefy back jerking with laughter. At least the Ghoulies, who were in beige camo gear, had followed the dress protocol.

Aliya glanced sideways at the other two Sweeper pods who, like them, sat tense on their carpets watching the wooden cupboard.

Now the music died down and the sphinxes retreated.

Aliya looked up as a familiar voice echoed over the square. Neon Ticker stood above them in a hovering whizzcalator with open doors. His hair this morning was bright white, matching his sleek suit. He looked suave and cheerful, as always. The approachable Council member, the one who always smiled, who was on the people's side, who calmed them when something bad happened. That was who he was on the surface, but now, as Aliya saw him standing there, glittering like a Christmas ornament, some gaudy angel hung up for everyone to see, she felt her stomach lurch. If Neon got his way, all these people he was smiling at in this square would perish.

'Dearly beloved,' Neon began. 'We have gathered here today to kick off our biennial flying carpet race through time, the Great Race. Are you all excited?'

Aliya exchanged a dark glance with Mustafa. There was a mixed response from the crowd, some cheering, while others booed. Not everyone thought the race going ahead was a good idea.

'Any moment now, our dear Miss Prim will fire the cannon and our pods will be off. Best of luck to the competitors,' Neon continued. 'May the superior team win.' He paused. 'Because we know that they must, and will.'

And there it was – a knowing smile spread across his face. His eyes glittered. He wasn't only speaking about the race pods. He meant them, the Loopers. They were superior and were going to win. That was the 'team' he was referring to.

'The scariest thing is that we don't know who we

can trust,' Mustafa whispered, leaning in. 'Anyone could be a Looper . . . the staff, or students.'

In front of them, Mr Blot had appeared next to the portal. Opening the first gateway was usually the job of a locksmith. The chief archivist blinked in the morning sun. He looked odd, Aliya thought, out here in the open air. With his mouse-brown cardigan, creased shirt and duster stuck under one arm, he looked like a creature that belonged between shelves, under the glare of a light bulb.

'He has most certainly sent out search parties to look for Aliya,' Victoria said with a nod at Neon. 'We mustn't talk to anyone . . . not even the Night Folk.'

'Or else we'll end up back at the Grizzled Hen under house arrest,' Aliya added.

'And don't take off your smartsuits . . . ever.' Victoria turned to Aliya. 'And—'

'I know, control my bird. She can't do much harm like this, can she?' Aliya gestured up at the invisible Simi on her shoulder. Victoria frowned.

Boom!

The air vibrated with the sound of the cannon

firing. The carpet twitched under Aliya, throwing her and the pod off balance. In front of them, Mr Blot had pulled open the portal door and the three race pods were swooshing towards it, the other Sweepers tailing them. High above the square, a great screen-carpet showed the pods whooshing through the portal. Film crews of genies and pixies followed in their wake, on carpets packed with recording equipment.

'Let's go!' Victoria cried, prodding Aliya to get the carpet started. 'Come on!'

It only took a light tap from Aliya with the special bamboo rod Professor Kashmir had given them to get Marauder going. The carpet accelerated rapidly and Aliya held her breath as they zoomed through the portal.

Chapter 11
MISR

It didn't take long for Aliya and the others to realize that they weren't in the human realm any more. Once they had passed through the portal and left the Citadel behind, they entered a busy market street that looked pretty much like the Khan el Khalili Bazaar Aliya remembered from back home in Cairo, except that there were stalls selling blue tobacco, lollipop gizzards, crunchy cockroach snacks and something that looked like candied toenails. Turning, Aliya saw that the portal they had come through was a decrepit shed with a sign reading: *Ghoul Latrine*.

'You are *off course*,' the knowledge turban hissed into Aliya's ear. 'Return to the race at once!'

'It wasn't us!' Aliya protested, feeling the velvety folds tighten around her head. 'This is where the portal took us!'

But to the turban it seemed not to matter *how* they had got where they were, only that they were in the wrong place. That, it concluded, was *their* fault. Aliya remembered that Miss Prim worked part-time educating knowledge turbans. Judging from the accusing tone, this one could very well be one of hers.

'Could you please tell us where we are?' Aliya asked it, as they zoomed along the bazaar.

'You are in Misr,' the turban continued, close to hysteria. 'A parallel dimension to Cairo, a similar city, only inhabited mostly by genies, but also home to a range of other mythicals.'

Misr. Aliya had read about it in her grandfather's books on Arabian folklore. She had also heard about it from Mr Kamel, who had grown up here. Perhaps this should have eased Aliya's worries, but she remembered that Kamel's stories about this outlandish place always ended by him telling her that it wasn't safe for humans. They might, as he put it, get 'unhinged' if they stayed too long. Aliya wasn't sure why that was, but she had a hunch. Once, during a video call with Mr Kamel, there had been genie children in the background playing marbles . . . using their heads to roll.

Aliya turned in her seat to consult with the others, but now the knowledge turban was working itself into such a frenzy on her head, shouting about trespassing and breaking the rules, that it was becoming impossible to form a coherent thought. Aliya tore it off and stuffed it into her satchel.

'This can't be the right place,' she said to the others. 'What do we do now?'

'I don't know,' Fuad said. He paused as a group of nasty-looking ifrit genies passed by under them. One of them reached up and traced its clawed fingers along Marauder's edge.

'My stealth sense tells me we need to get out of this crowded street,' Fuad continued. 'We need to hide . . . fast.'

'The Loopers must have diverted the course,' Victoria said when they were sheltering on the rooftop of a decrepit bathhouse. 'Or is this it?'

Around them, Misr spread out, a colourful jumble of housetops and pillars of rising smoke. The sun was high and dust danced in the air.

'But humans aren't allowed here,' Mustafa said. 'This is mythical territory, and a wild place. And if they discover that we're travellers, it might be even worse. The mythicals here don't generally approve of our Reform and Civilization programme. Making them safe for humans to be around is not really in their interest. They feel it's like clipping their wings. I can't imagine how the Council would approve the course to go through here.'

Mustafa had mentioned Misr to them before. He'd met mythicals at the Refuge who, in search of a safer life, had fled from it to the Infinitum.

Aliya looked down at the street below, at the steady flow of peculiar and scary-looking creatures. No wonder Mr Kamel had never brought her or Geddo here to visit. Maybe his stories of the steakhouses serving human shish kebabs had not just been made up to scare her . . .

'This is Neon's doing, obviously,' she said. 'We're not in the proper race any more.'

Aliya turned her attention to the nadim on her shoulder. Simi was tense and, in a sudden surge, Aliya got a sense of the danger she felt. Also, her invisibility cream was wearing off. Lifting the hoopoe from her shoulder to her wrist, she could see her faintly. It was like looking at something through a smudged lens.

'My tracker can't read the terrain,' Victoria said, frowning over her astrolabe. 'It's like the signals are disturbed. What about the smoke bracelet?'

Aliya held up her wrist to show the others the thin sliver of smoke that hung coiled around it.

'Nothing yet.'

'You said it was supposed to guide us to the locksmiths!' Victoria barked. 'So why isn't it working?'

Aliya was about to come up with an excuse when Karima began waving.

'Look!' She pointed into the street below. 'Down there!'

Below them in the street were the Janissaries, zigzagging through the stalls.

'We've got to tell them the race's been sabotaged,' Victoria said. 'Come on, let's catch up.'

'But stealthily,' Fuad said. 'Aion, pure invisibility mode.'

Aion fiddled with her remote. A moment later Aliya felt her smartsuit heating up. Something was happening. Next to her, Victoria was transforming too.

'What in all of Bloomingdale's have you done?' Victoria cried, looking down at her hands. They had turned wrinkled and slightly green, or her smartgloves had.

Aliya yelped as Victoria's face turned old, creased and light green. The rest of her pod had also transformed.

'We're a group of old genies on a trip to the city to sell cats,' Aion explained. Looking down, Aliya realized that her satchel now looked like it was bulging with fur.

'You like the storyline?' Aion continued. 'I just thought of it.'

'No one sells cats!' Victoria screeched. 'What kind of cover is that?'

After a short argument, Aion, who loved cats, was persuaded to change their fictional goods to green, broccoli-smelling tobacco, like the type Mr Kamel smoked – the only kind of mythical ware they could think of.

'Blend in,' Victoria commanded as Aliya got Marauder started again. 'And act like genies, for God's sake.'

Aliya wasn't exactly sure how a genie was supposed to act. The one she knew the best was Mr Kamel, so she tried to look superior as she steered the carpet the way the Janissaries had gone. But, because of their delay getting transformed and arguing about cats, the senior pod was no longer visible.

With so many new, weird things around them, it was hard to focus as they flew through the bazaar, especially for Mustafa, who had read about many of the mythical creatures they came across, but never seen them in real life. There were dulhaths (ostrich genies) and the very peculiar aksars – a monster with the head of an ox, the antlers of a stag and the hindquarters of a big cat.

'There they are!' Aliya cried, pointing to the far end of the alley where it opened up on to a square. As they neared, they saw the Janissaries hovering in front of the entrance of a run-down coffee house. A couple of wildermen were sitting at a rickety table outside, playing some board games with pawns that looked like cockroaches. Their grimy beards hung all the way to their knees.

'Wildermen are very rare,' Mustafa explained excitedly, as they rose up to hover above the square. 'They live in packs in the deepest recesses of the Infinitum Wilderness, hence the name.' He sounded like a naturalist on TV who had just come across some near-extinct species in the jungle. 'Expeditions have been made to search and study them, but they've resisted all attempts to be civilized. They have a fondness for human clothes, though, and travellers living at the outskirts of the Citadel have reported that wildermen sometimes steal clothes off their washing lines. Anyway, the Council eventually left them alone. Since they don't use magic, they pose no real threat to us travellers. They are part desert giant, though, so we should keep our distance.'

'That and the stink!' Victoria pinched her nose closed in disgust. Aliya could smell it too. The pong of unwashed clothes and beards was drifting towards them on the wind.

'It looks like they've found a portal. Hopefully a way out of here,' Victoria said, pointing at the pod, who were hovering right outside the coffee house's latrine. 'We'll approach slowly.'

Bulbul Baki, the Janissaries' navigator, had jumped off their carpet and was sticking his travel key in the door lock. There was a pulse of light from within, nothing an untrained eye would notice.

As the door opened, a black gust surged through the doorway and relentlessly sucked at the young travellers. Aliya winced as Victoria took a pincer grip on her arm. They watched in horror as the race pod struggled against the dark substance.

'We have to help them!' Aliya cried. She was about to give Marauder the command to descend, but Victoria stopped her.

'No one move,' she said. 'We don't know what we're up against.'

'She's right,' Fuad said. 'If we go any closer, that . . . thing will eat us too.'

'It's the Shop.' Aliya shook her head. Tears were

beginning to rise in her eyes. She wiped them away with the back of her wrinkly genie hand. 'Look.'

Things had begun to spill out of the darkness. A deluge of random items – things that shouldn't be moving – rushed over the pod, hiding them from sight. Teapots, forks and jabbing knives. Walking statues, animated accordions, toasters, shoes, lamps, stuffed animals all conspired to drag the struggling pod through the opening.

'They're cursed objects from the Shop of Second Chances,' Aliya said when the pod and the paraphernalia had disappeared and the portal had closed once more, by itself. 'Dorian and the Loopers must have booby-trapped the racecourse.'

Around them, the activity in the square had not changed. The wildermen were still moving cockroaches around on their board. Aliya wondered if they had looked up even once while the scene was playing out.

'What will happen to them?' Karima asked, in a faint voice. She looked as shaken as Aliya felt. 'Will they be . . .' She shook her head as if the words were too hard to pronounce. 'You know . . .'

'Not killed, no,' Aliya said. 'Something worse. The Shop's magic feeds on life energy, so unless we do something to help them, they'll probably end up feeding it by turning into one of those cursed objects.'

At that moment, the smoke bracelet Nigm had left for her unfurled, shaped itself into an arrow and pointed away across the rooftops.

'About time.' Aliya wiped her eyes. 'Come on. We need to go that way!' The smoky arrow was pointing east.

'So, the locksmiths did pass through here?' Mustafa asked.

Aliya shrugged.

'We'll soon find out.'

Out of the corner of her eye, she saw the wildermen stand up. Their creepy board game fell with a crash and a rattle to the ground.

'But the course is booby-trapped,' Karima said. 'Any one of the portals we're guided to might lead to the Shop. How will we know which is safe?'

'We don't,' Aliya said. 'But the locksmiths only have so much time before they disintegrate and die, remember. We've *got* to continue searching for them.'

Ahead of them, the smoke arrow hung suspended, waiting for them to follow.

Just then, Marauder jerked violently sideways and began to sink. A rusty hook had attached to one of the carpet's front corners, causing it to nosedive. Below them stood the wildermen, hauling them in, Marauder at the end of a rope like a large kite.

'Don't panic,' Mustafa said as they neared ground level. 'Wildermen are supposed to be peaceful creatures. They're probably just curious. I'm sure they are more reasonable than they are . . . groomed.' He smiled, eyes bright with fear, as they reached eye level with the mythicals.

'Hello there, good sir,' Mustafa said. 'How can we help you?'

The nearest wilderman moved closer, grinning. His friend was approaching too, combing his grimy beard with long-nailed fingers. Up close, with their beards and their dirty plaid shirts, they looked like a pair of mouldy lumberjacks.

'Unhand the carpet, sir,' Victoria tried. 'We are

simple broccoli salespeople—'

'Tobacco,' Aliya hissed.

'Tobacco salespeople . . . and very old genies, as you can see.'

In front of them, the wilderman was simply staring at them with his mouth open. Victoria sounded much too posh to be a tobacco salesperson and why, Aliya thought, had she added that thing about being 'very old'?

'Um, I'm not sure he's buying it,' Mustafa whispered through a frozen smile. 'I wish I had my books with me, so I could look up—'

'Tobacco, eh?' said a high-pitched voice. The next moment, there was a rustle in the wilderman's beard and a small creature looked out – a squirrel with red eyes. 'If that's tobacco,' it said, pointing at the holographic heap in Aliya's satchel, 'I'm the Queen of Sweden.'

'It's a talking squirrel,' Mustafa said. Aliya could almost hear how his brain tried to place it within his catalogue of mythical creatures.

'That's not a real squirrel,' she muttered. 'It's possessed. Must be from the Shop as well.'

The squirrel turned its creepy eyes on her.

'We've been promised a juicy reward if we were to capture a group of young time-travellers.' The small animal hauled itself a little higher in the wilderman's beard. 'You haven't happened to see such a group, have you?'

'No, not at all,' said Fuad, making his voice deep. 'We're just a bunch of old tobacco sellers—'

'Sure.' The squirrel whistled through its front teeth. 'Now, why don't you come with us in a nice and orderly fashion to the portal over there, just like all the others?' It pointed to the door through which the Janissaries had just disappeared. 'Or will Cute-and-Cuddly here have to convince you?'

He jabbed his little squirrel fist in the largest wilderman's direction.

'What do you mean "all the others"?' Karima asked.

'Show them,' the squirrel ordered. The wilderman pulled out part of a pink overall.

'The Philosophers,' Aliya whispered, aghast. 'They've got them too!'

The wilderman continued to empty his pockets. This time he hauled out a smashed-up camera.

'A news team!' Karima yelped.

'I'm afraid your disguises aren't any good to someone equipped with magic.' The squirrel tapped the side of its head. 'It's in my eyes, see? Escape is futile. The whole town is looking for you.'

The children exchanged horrified glances.

'How many pods have you . . . caught so far?' Aliya asked, fishing for what could've happened to the Ghoulies and the Sweepers.

'Four,' the squirrel said. 'And that's just us. Now come along.'

The squirrel gave a sharp whistle and one of the wildermen gave Marauder a fierce tug. Next thing Aliya knew, he had a clamp-like hold on her arm. His friend didn't waste any time either, grabbing hold of Victoria, who shrieked like a banshee, and Karima, who began throwing punches.

'It's better you don't resist,' the squirrel said. 'Or Cute-and-Cuddly might break some bones. Not that it isn't something they enjoy.'

Within moments, the wildermen had folded the carpet around the children and were dragging them along.

'Marauder, fly!' Aliya screeched from inside the cramped darkness, her limbs all bunched up in an uncomfortable squeeze with the rest of the pod's. The carpet lunged sideways. Aliya felt herself slam against something hard – probably a wall – then felt Marauder struggle to get free, squeezing her and the others even tighter together. This was not the first time she had been squeezed by a carpet, but it was definitely the worst.

'Arghh!' Victoria groaned into Aliya's armpit. 'Somebody *do* something!'

Aliya was getting faint from the lack of air.

'Fly, Marauder!' she begged. 'Fly!'

The large carpet struggled against the big fists that held it. Finally, with a great heave, they shot upwards, bouncing against a wall before they soared up into the sky.

As Marauder unfolded, Aliya saw that the wilderman with the squirrel was still hanging off the side of the carpet, weighing it down so much that he was dragging them back towards the ground. 'That's right!' the squirrel hollered from its place in the beard. 'Pull it down! Crash it!'

Aliya could feel Marauder growing tired. It could only be seconds before they plummeted to the ground.

'Take that, you horrid brute!' Victoria screamed, swinging her satchel at the wilderman's head.

He dodged the blow and reached out to grab her, but then something strange happened. The big man began to scream. The children looked on in surprise, all except Aion, who was fiddling with a jar. Pouring out of it were minuscule black creepy-crawlies with long legs, running down the carpet and disappearing into the wilderman's clothes.

Spiders.

With a scream of fury, the possessed squirrel fell towards the ground as his wilderman let go. Marauder could finally rise into the air, away from the ground and danger.

'Pickled frogs! What just happened?' Karima asked Aion when they had landed on a nearby roof, exhausted and winded.

'They're called *spiders*,' Aion said, smiling, waving the glass jar. 'Cool, right?'

'You mean they're not some sort of holographics?' Fuad asked.

Aion nodded. 'They're extinct in my time, but I've been growing some in my room.'

Fuad burst out laughing and the others, shaken but relieved, dared to smile.

Aliya felt for Simi who, during the squeeze and tumble inside the carpet, had transformed into a key – the shape she usually took when things went sideways. She eased the nadim out from where she'd hidden inside her collar and tucked her into a breast pocket for safekeeping.

'Our disguises,' she said, noticing the suit fabric. 'They've disappeared.'

And yes, their smartsuits were back to standby mode, looking like ordinary grey overalls. From neighbouring buildings, she could already see curious eyes peering at them from dark windows. With the sunlight catching the plain fabric, they were more visible than ever.

'Start them up again,' Victoria commanded Aion. 'Hurry. The whole town is searching for us, remember?'

Aion held up the control panel that worked the smartsuits. It was cracked clean in half.

'It happened during the fight with the hairy men,' she explained.

More faces were appearing at windows, some recognizable creatures Aliya had encountered at the Citadel. Others she had never seen before, not even in her grandfather's or Mustafa's books, like the bald half-man who now hopped across the roof closest to them. He had only one leg and one arm, on opposite sides of his body.

'That's a nasnas,' Mustafa said, his voice choked with terror. 'We've got to get out of here, quick. A touch from that creature would be enough to kill us.'

'But to *where?*' Karima asked. She too looked scared, and she had every right to be. Glancing about them, Aliya saw more creatures were approaching. Genies, ghouls, silas . . . and not the fairly tame ones they knew from the Citadel. These were rough and menacing. The stuff of nightmares.

'That way,' Aliya said, pointing past a monster who was carrying his bald head under his arm, at where the smoke arrow had reshaped in the air ahead of them. 'That's where the locksmiths went.'

They flew in silence, clinging to each other, only

now and then glancing down to see if they were being followed. Everywhere they passed, mythicals stopped and looked up as if they could sense them – smell them – and knew they didn't belong, and maybe, that there was a bounty on their heads. The headless monster was following on the ground, his arms lifting his detached head high to search for them. Other creatures joined in the hunt too, until a horde were in pursuit, like a monstrous tail.

By the time they flew into a quieter, more sparsely populated part of Misr, a veritable mob was following them. Zoureg snakes, more wildermen and silas, their weather constellations whipping up the air as the crowd pressed through the streets in pursuit.

'Hurry!' Karima shouted from her place at the back. 'We've got to speed up!'

'There!' Aliya pointed across the street at a building made entirely out of black bricks. 'That's where the arrow is pointing.' The smoke was hovering lightly in the air just ahead of the carpet, and was unmistakably aiming at the building. 'That must be where Nigm went.'

Above the door was a glittering sign that read

Hall of Mirrors in an elegant cursive. *A place of truths*, read a line underneath the name.

'A hall of mirrors?' Victoria said. 'That sounds like a trap, for sure. Plus, the mob's going to follow us inside!'

'It might be just the place to buy us the time we need to get out of here,' Aion said. She nodded at Aliya. 'You're a locksmith, aren't you. You can open a new portal.'

Aliya stared at her. 'I'm not sure—'

'You did it last time, when we escaped from the Grizzled Hen,' Aion insisted. 'And it worked.'

'So what if we end up in a fuul shop or in some ladies' changing room?' Victoria cried. 'Even a Mongol raid is better than the Shop, isn't it?'

Aliya clutched Simi through the fabric of her breast pocket. If only the nadim would take them to one of those places, rather than leading them straight into what they were running away from. But Aliya also knew it wasn't just down to her nadim – if they ended up in the Shop, it would be just as much her fault.

Chapter 12
THE HALL OF MIRRORS

Marauder dove across the street and into the hall of mirrors. They shot through the black curtains that hung just inside the open front door, shielding the interior from view. On the other side was an overwhelmingly red foyer. The wall-to-wall carpet was a deep blood red, as were the two armchairs on one side and to the front of the ticket booth. Looking around, Aliya felt a jab of unease – a feeling she saw reflected in the faces of her friends. There was something about this place, from the glittering sign to the fact that the entrance was abandoned, that did not bode well. But in this situation, it was an escape of sorts, at least for the short time Aliya would need to gather herself and attempt to open a portal to escape properly. Now the sound of grunts, shouts and heavy footsteps reached them from outside. The mob was coming. They had no time to lose.

'Where do we go?' Aliya turned to the others.

'There!' Victoria pointed to a black door.

Marauder hesitated by the doorway, his edges too large to fit. The children quickly slid off and pushed through the opening, the carpet following, edges tucked in.

They stepped into a white mist and looked around to see a perfectly round room, with mirrors for walls. Once the door behind them closed, it merged with the rest of the glass like a portal closing. In the mirrors, they saw themselves reflected into a kaleidoscope of faces, arms, torsos. Aliya felt her head swim and backed up against a cold sheet of glass, just to feel something solid. The mist was probing her, like an inquisitive entity, coiling around her neck, humming in her ears, and something tensed inside her – a feeling that she couldn't define. She looked around for the others, the sense of urgency and disorientation growing stronger with each passing moment, and saw her friends, thousands of them, reflected in the surrounding mirrors. For minutes, hours – Aliya wasn't sure which – she gazed groggily at the moving reflections of her friends. Which one was real?

Then someone was tugging at her arm, hard. It was Victoria.

'See what you did?' she spat, her eyes strangely glazed. 'You're always getting us into trouble. You and your locksmith ways. All your secrets. It's your fault we're in this mess. You've been sabotaging this pod since the day you joined.'

Aliya knew that she shouldn't react, that there was something about this mist that was affecting their minds, yet the tension inside her chest was so strong, she had to let it out. *A place of truths*, the sign outside had read. Maybe this was what the mist wanted . . . for her to speak the truth.

'Don't you talk to me about secrets,' she cried at the many images of her podmates. 'You're supposed to be my team, but ever since the term started you're nowhere to be found. I'm always having breakfast alone, dinner alone because you're rushing off to . . .

well, I don't know, do I? Because I'm apparently not important enough to share stuff with!

'And you?' She turned to the images of Karima that swam above her. 'I thought we were best friends, but you wouldn't even help me save my grandfather and now he's . . . he's—'

She couldn't say it. Not even here in this place of truths. She was supposed to apologize to her friend, but she couldn't. It hurt too much.

'Aliya,' Karima began, her soft face infinitely replicated and contorted with sadness. 'If there was any way of saving your grandfather, Matron and I would have—'

'You're wrong!' Aliya shouted. 'You're all wrong!' She turned and began groping for a way out. 'What do you or Matron know? You just gave up! On him and me and . . . You know what, I've got to get out of here.'

She pushed against the glass behind her until one slab gave way and allowed her to slip through, but only stepped into more brightness and mist. Behind her, she heard Mustafa calling her name, urging her to come back, but she kept on. For some minutes she walked, dazed, through the mist and mirrors.

Finally, resting against a wall, Aliya discerned a maze through the white haze, all white walls and doors, but no reflecting glass. Panic sucked at her, but she forced it down. The smoky arrow had again become a bracelet curled around her wrist. Why had it stopped showing the way? Was it as confused as she was by this place – the mist, the maze?

Now she heard the sound of voices. Resisting an urge to call out for her friends, she crouched down and waited. There was no telling who else could be moving around in this strange place.

Two figures were coming towards her through the mist. As they neared, Aliya saw that they were the exact same height and bulky shape. First one and then the other burst out laughing. It was a wild, raucous laughter that Aliya would have recognized anywhere: Salman Bashiri, the Ghoulies' navigator. But there were *two* of him, walking close together, their muscular arms hooked.

Aliya, who for a moment had been relieved at the sight of a familiar face, thinking that the Ghoulies at least might be safe, shrank back against the wall.

There was something terribly wrong going on. What kind of hall of mirrors was this that *doubled* people?

'I'll hold them down and you'll hit,' one of the Salmans said to the other as they passed. 'Punch them to pulp.'

'They'll never see us coming,' said the other, swinging a large fist. Aliya couldn't see either of their faces clearly, but she could sense the grins, the strange excitement in their movements.

'They'll see us coming twice,' said the first, and they burst out laughing again, but not in Salman's good-natured way. This laugh was wild and cruel.

Aliya sat frozen after they had passed, not daring to move. Voices and laughter echoed through the maze, drifting past in the mist. The strange acoustics, or maybe it was the mist itself, made it impossible to discern if the sounds were right up close or far away. Why had she left her friends? Had it been the mist? Regardless of their disagreements, she'd never before questioned their need to stay together as a group. And yet she'd done just that. Her rage, her disappointment . . . it had swelled in that mist into something too big to push back down.

Just like the mirrors had multiplied their images, the mist had intensified her feelings. *This*, Aliya concluded where she sat huddled, *is a really evil place*.

She had begun to walk along the wall in the opposite direction from Salman and his double, listening for any sign of her friends, when new figures appeared. It was one of the parties of news genies and pixies this time – a whole horde, since they too were doubled. But unlike Salman, they were at war with themselves, bickering and pinching and pulling at each other's hair and wings – a mess of chattering creatures, too busy with their quarrel to pay her any mind.

Aliya continued walking, too restless and heartsick to stay still. She had the horrible feeling that something was following her in the mist, just out of sight.

She lost track of time. Had she walked for minutes or hours? She wasn't sure. At last, too exhausted to take another step, she sank down at an intersection to rest. It was not long before she felt that whatever had been following her was there, just steps away.

'I don't care who you are!' she shouted into the

mist. 'I'll melt your face off!'

Frowning in concentration, she tried to summon her locksmith powers. But when the figure came nearer, she lost focus. There in the mist was . . . herself. It was she – her tousled hair, her slightly crooked nose, her hazel eyes.

The figure walked up to her, then sank down on its haunches opposite Aliya, mirroring her. Aliya drew back and stood up. The mirror image followed suit.

'Who are you?' Aliya asked, pressing herself backwards into the wall. There was something terrifying about looking yourself in the eyes – about seeing something you *were* and yet knew so little about.

'I'm you, silly,' the other her said with a wry smile. 'I'm a mirror. Didn't you read the sign outside?'

Aliya frowned in confusion. This was not the kind of hall of mirrors she had seen in movies, at fairgrounds, with special glass that made one look shorter or fatter or turned upside down.

'Are you real?' Aliya asked, resisting the temptation to touch the other her, to feel if she was solid.

'In here I am,' the other her said. 'Now, come on. What would you like to do? Some go mad and want to destroy things . . . others just cry. It varies a lot from person to person. It's the mist, you know. It lifts our pretence of being civilized. Gets us back to the bedrock of being.'

Aliya thought of Salman, how feral he had become in here. He was a troll, after all. And the reporter pixies and genies – they too had succumbed to something raw and unfiltered. They might have been chased in here, just like her pod had been, until they got trapped in the mist.

'You don't look like the vicious type, though,' said the other her. 'I do sense guilt, however. Lots of guilt.' The other self pressed closer. 'We could hurt ourselves, if you like? Might that feel good?'

'No!' Aliya backed away. 'Don't touch me!'

'All right, all right.' The other her gestured at the room around her, at a white door just visible through the light mist. 'Then let's do something fun. We like adventure. I can sense that. Go ahead, open the door. Takes you wherever you like for a quarter of an hour. You pay extra if you want to stay longer. Most people do.'

'But we didn't pay anything to get in,' Aliya said.

'I didn't say you pay money.' The other her looked amused. A chill travelled up Aliya's spine.

'I'd like to find my friends,' she said, looking around. Claustrophobia surged through her. Could they be on the other side of the door? Should she try opening one or would it lead to a trap? In her pocket, Simi was still in her key shape, pulsing slightly and getting hotter and hotter, sensing Aliya's fear.

'Don't worry,' the other her said. 'I'll open it. All you have to do is watch.'

Before Aliya had formed a plan of action, the other her had pulled the door open. On the other side Aliya saw her pod's common room, with its squashy armchairs covered in Matron Olfat's attempts at crochet. There was a fire burning in the hearth. On the rickety coffee table stood a silver tray loaded with all of Mrs Dickens's best treats: moist slices of date cake, shortbread and petits fours. As the warmth from the fire wafted towards her, she realized how cold she was. Chilled to the bone, in fact, and dying to step into this room, which was the most familiar place to her in both the earthly and

Infinitum sphere.

'Go on,' the other her said. 'Just step through.'

Aliya had put one foot through the door when something grabbed her around the ankle. She could not see what it was, but felt it tug her ferociously towards the room. From behind, the other her was pushing. A howl rose from her throat as she gripped the doorway to keep from getting forced through.

'Let me go!' she screamed. Closing her eyes, Aliya summoned her locksmith powers, feeling the energy pool in her palms. Turning, she managed to slap the doppelganger, but it melted away like quicksand only to reshape again.

'You're too bogged down with guilt to get past me,' the other her panted. 'Too full of regrets, too much in your head. It's time you make up your mind about magic. Come on, join us. You know we can save your grandfather.' It laughed and grasped at her. Aliya couldn't get free.

She was almost through the doorway when something tugged her backwards, away from the room. Mustafa was behind her, red in the face, screaming furiously at the other her and pulling. For a few seconds, his appearance stunned Aliya so much that she forgot to struggle. She had never seen Mustafa screaming, or furious. Their eyes met for a moment. *What are you doing?* Mustafa's eyes said. *Fight*. Snapped out of her trance, Aliya began to struggle for real . . .

She fought with every last bit of strength in her body. Even Simi transformed into a hoopoe that emerged from Aliya's breast pocket to peck at the menacing figure. Finally overpowered, the other her let go and sank into the opening that had shed its illusion to show them what it really was. Beyond the doorway was the dirty, cluttered front room of the Shop of Second Chances. With a last screech, the other her finally let go and sank away into the Shop. Mustafa quickly pulled the door shut.

'How did you find me?' Aliya sank down on her haunches, trying not to throw up. The shock and terror were turning the corridor into a blur.

'The lights from your palms,' Mustafa said. 'I got separated from the others in the mist and followed it here.'

'All those doors must have been rigged to lead to

the Shop too,' Aliya said, leaning weakly against the wall. 'They've probably booby-trapped every single doorway in Misr.' She stroked Simi, who was pulsing with a worried glow.

They hurried down the corridor, shouting for the others, turning one corner after the other without any luck, until they both began to suspect that the maze was somehow alive, shifting around them, and had no intention of bringing them together with their friends.

'I met myself too,' Mustafa panted as they walked. 'It kept wailing and clinging to me. It was horrible.'

Then, as they stood catching their breath, they noticed a new mist seeping in through the walls. The magic was back. A place in the wall opposite began to crackle, as if something was forcing itself through.

'Open a portal,' Mustafa said, rigid with horror. 'Quickly, before it starts over.'

'I can't guarantee anything, but—'

'You've got to,' Mustafa finished. 'Or we're done for.'

They ran down the corridor, turning right and

left until they came upon a door.

Please, Aliya thought as she stroked Simi, urging her to transform. *Let this work*. To her relief, the nadim did not protest, but again turned into her key shape. She too must have feared and hated this place.

Slipping Simi into the lock, she thought about the common room again, back at the hostel – the real one this time. That was where she wanted to go, to where Geddo was, and Matron Olfat and maybe Mr Kamel – adults who could protect her and make everything all right.

She felt Simi pulse in her hand. Opening her eyes, Aliya saw that the door had clicked open to a hallway. There was a wooden cabinet, a chair, a hall table, a hat stand, a potted plant. She sighed in relief. It wasn't the common room back at the hostel, but at least it wasn't the Shop. It looked safe enough. She tentatively stuck her hand through and touched the cool floorboards. No magic.

'Any idea where this is?' Mustafa asked.

She shook her head, but there was not a moment to waste. The mist was upon them again and with it came a horde of formless white entities who, as they neared, began to take shape . . . their shapes.

'Go!' Mustafa cried. They quickly pushed through the opening, leaving the mist and their doubles behind.

Once on the other side, Aliya reverse-locked, closing the portal.

'Phew,' Mustafa said. 'That was close.'

That was when the ground gave way, and they began to fall.

Chapter 13
THE GUARDIAN OF THE IN-BETWEEN

They plummeted downwards. Around them was the darkness of space, but all the furniture they had found in the hallway was still there and falling with them, just like something out of *Alice in Wonderland*. Aliya clung hopelessly to the top of the hat stand. Mustafa was cradling the potted fern.

Before they had time to despair, a lady appeared, sitting in the chair next to the falling hall table. She had startlingly red, henna-dyed hair that lifted off her shoulders as the armchair fell. But this didn't seem to bother her. She was, in fact, busy painting her nails. The bottle of nail polish was falling right alongside the armchair with everything else. Aliya stared as the woman screwed the top shut and examined her handiwork.

'I'm Hafiza,' she said at length. 'Welcome to the space-time glitch, or the in-between, as some call it.'

'Space-time glitch?' Aliya mumbled, her mouth drier than desert sand. She returned Mustafa's look of horror.

'Tea?' asked Hafiza casually, opening the falling cabinet and taking out a teapot. She nodded at Mustafa who stared back at her.

'No?' The lady turned to Aliya. 'Just a drop?'

Aliya managed to shrug. She watched as the lady brought out a jug of milk, sugar cubes and a plate of biscuits, all of which were placed on the table that was falling near her. Their descent, which had begun like a free-fall, had gradually slowed until they were drifting downwards. There was something soothing about the way they floated, and Aliya, still raw from the fight with the pod and the struggle with the other her, felt a momentary relief. The situation was odd enough to distract her.

'Shall I be mother?' Hafiza asked as she lifted the pot. To Aliya's surprise, it contained hot tea. She nodded stupidly.

'I've been expecting you,' Hafiza said as she handed Aliya a cup. The contents immediately splashed away into the air, passing Aliya's head like a liquid cloud. 'It didn't take long for you to show up.'

'How did you know we'd be here?' Aliya asked breathlessly, watching her teacup and saucer float away.

Hafiza sipped her tea which, for some reason, stayed put in her cup. Reaching into her sleeve, she pulled out a photograph and flicked it at Aliya who, as it swirled past her head, widened her eyes in surprise. She had caught a glimpse of a tall, sharp-nosed figure dressed from top to toe in tweed.

'*Mr Kamel* asked you?'

'We're related,' Hafiza said. 'Can't remember how, exactly. Something about an uncle who married a genie. Also, I'm Night Folk. I was asked to keep a lookout for you from between the worlds.'

Aliya exchanged another glance with Mustafa.

'Don't worry,' Hafiza said. 'I'm not going to have you sent back to the Grizzled Hen.'

'It's an honour to meet you,' said Mustafa who

was now falling upside down and had begun to look fascinated. 'You – you are a hafiz, aren't you? A guardian of the in-between?'

'My name gives it away, doesn't it?' Hafiza said. 'That and my command of gravity.'

'Could we please stop falling?' Aliya whimpered. She was beginning to feel sick, and she didn't want to find out what vomiting would be like in the in-between.

'I guess I shouldn't have pulled you through the glitch,' Hafiza said. 'Just easier to shake off magic that way. It tends to cling. All right.'

She clapped her hands together and suddenly they weren't falling any more. Aliya felt a floor come up to meet her and she thudded to the ground, feet first. Thankfully, the floor was covered in a thick rug, which cushioned the impact. Yet suddenly having something solid under her feet was too much of a shock for her shaken body, and she fell over like a chopped tree. Mustafa lay on the floor next to her, like a piece of wilted salad.

'I never want to do that again,' he groaned, his cheek pressed into the carpet.

Sitting up, Aliya looked around. They were in a round room that looked like a cross between an observatory and a kitchen. It had a polished wooden floor and white wool rugs. The furniture was comfortable and simple. A panoramic window spanned the length of the curved space.

'Don't throw up on the floor,' Hafiza said from where she now stood next to an ordinary-looking kitchen counter, making a fresh pot of tea. 'I just had it waxed.'

Aliya instinctively felt for Simi in her pocket. She was there, and in her key form. Aliya sighed in relief.

'I think we'd better try teatime again,' Hafiza said. 'Some food in the stomach will chase away the glitch sickness. When was the last time you ate?'

'Breakfast,' Aliya said weakly. Outside the window, it was night. Three moons hung like ripe fruits in the starry sky.

'I take it this isn't Earth,' Mustafa whispered. He, too, had discovered the additional planets.

'I call it the Outpost,' Hafiza said, pouring hot water into the pot. 'It's where I come to think things over.'

Aliya rubbed her face. What time was it here in this in-between place? The breakfast at the hostel that morning felt like a lifetime ago, and now that they were not falling or being chased, she could feel her stomach growling with hunger.

'Come on.' Hafiza set the steaming pot down on a wooden table. 'Let's eat.'

When they'd brought the food and were seated, Aliya stared into the tea Hafiza had poured for her. It smelt of honey and something minty. She hesitated for a moment, but then decided to drink. Hafiza was beyond odd, but she was related to Mr Kamel, affiliated with the Night Folk, and had pulled them out of Misr, a literal minefield of magic traps.

'It's really good,' she told Mustafa, who tried some too and brightened a little.

'It's made from the sound of frangipani flowers blossoming,' Hafiza said, pouring more tea into Mustafa's cup.

Aliya decided not to comment. Hafiza seemed just the sort of being who could make tea out of the sound of something, so in a way it was not surprising at all.

'Do you know where our friends are?' Aliya asked. The enormity of what had happened was beginning to sink in, and with it the terrible truth: they had been saved, but their friends . . . what had become of them?

'They're still alive.' Hafiza gave her a grave look. 'But the Loopers already got them.' Hafiza shook her head. 'I'm sorry.'

The children sat silently for some moments. Aliya felt the world begin to darken again. The others were alive but captured. What would the Loopers do to them? It didn't bear thinking about.

'It's not over yet,' Hafiza said. 'I thought you were on a rescue mission?'

'We are.' Aliya exchanged a glance with Mustafa. 'We've got to find the locksmiths. Only they can secure the Smithy and expose the Loopers' plan once and for all. Without the magic they're planning to source from the Sublimes, they're just a bunch of idiots in hoods.'

'So.' Hafiza blew on her tea. 'Not quite the moment to despair, then, is it?'

'You couldn't by any chance tell us where the

locksmiths are?' Mustafa asked hopefully.

'That's outside of my domain, I'm afraid. Besides, I've got many worlds to look after – an infinite number, in fact.' The guardian reached out to touch the smoke bracelet that hung around Aliya's wrist, a smoky sliver. 'But you've got a guide already. Now, it does no one any good worrying on an empty stomach. *Eat.*'

The rest of the spread was less esoteric, if just as mismatched as their plates. Hafiza evidently liked to do her shopping in different times – there were Roman stuffed dates, medieval fried fig tarts and spiced plum mousse, fifteenth-century goat and onion broth, Victorian apple snow and finally, Egyptian molokhiyya, hot and green, over rice mixed with vermicelli.

When they were thoroughly stuffed, they sat back, sipping their tea while Hafiza entertained them with stories of worlds they hadn't the slightest idea existed. She told of diplomatic missions in desert kingdoms with five suns and pink gazelles, of splendorous sky balls in worlds where the weak gravity allowed the natives to fly into space like helium balloons, and host cloud-sculpting parties.

'Would it really be possible for Neon to create a new world with magic?' Aliya asked at length.

'Perhaps,' Hafiza said. 'But magic is parasitic. It needs stolen life to get stronger. There would never be anything genuine or real about a world like that. Still, there have always been fanatics, like Dorian Darke and Neon Ticker, who believe that they will manage what no one else has.'

When the children were done cleaning up, they joined Hafiza at the panoramic window, where she stood looking through a large telescope. Outside a desert spread out, its dunes white and billowing in the moonlight. The three moons were hanging in the sky, along with a host of other planets Aliya had no idea what to call.

'Have a look.' She offered Aliya the telescope. Aliya felt a flutter in her heart as she looked through the eyepiece.

'Do you see them?' Hafiza asked. 'The doorways?'

Aliya blinked, her eyes tearing and then . . . what she had thought were stars were really pulsing spots of different colours, like the Northern Lights, sprinkled confetti-like across the velvety sky. There were so many, an infinite number.

'There's an opening into every moment in time, in every world,' Hafiza said.

'Every moment in every . . .' Mustafa's voice trailed off.

'That's a lot,' Aliya concluded.

Just then, the smoke bracelet around Aliya's wrist uncurled and became an arrow again, pointing to the sky.

'If we could find the *right* portal,' Aliya asked Hafiza, 'could you get us through it?'

'I'm quite good with *coulds*,' said the guardian.

The smoke arrow hovered in front of them, impatiently prodding at the panoramic window.

'I suppose you'd better take my carpets,' Hafiza continued. 'Not sure you would survive the zip. Last time I took a guest zipping, only his upper half came along.'

Mustafa shot Aliya a horrified glance.

Aliya's heart pinched as she thought of Marauder, the Persian carpet. He too had been lost in the hall of mirrors.

They watched as Hafiza tapped the fringe of two of the white wool rugs, which sleepily rose in the air and drifted towards them.

'I won't be able to guarantee your safety once you walk through the portal,' Hafiza said when they were seated and ready to go, the children each on one of the wool rugs. 'But these carpets will get you there.' With a swipe of a hand, she set the exit door in motion. It opened with a soft whirr.

They drifted out of the Outpost and into the night air. Aliya's head swam as she looked down. Below, the desert stretched out. Above, the night sky seemed just as infinite.

'How are we ever going to reach the right portal?' Mustafa asked anxiously.

'*You* can't, obviously,' Hafiza said. She had seated herself at the back of her own carpet, a round, long-haired affair.

'But then how . . . ?' Mustafa looked from Hafiza to the smoke arrow that was gliding ahead, slowly but surely, following its invisible trail.

'Here, smoky.' Hafiza held out her index finger. The arrow made a polite turn and wrapped its tail around Hafiza's fingertip. 'All right. Hold on to your—'

On the word 'heads', the party shot forward. They flew at lightning speed, so fast that everything around them became a blur. Aliya thought the sensation was similar to going through the Whoosh, the sort-of customs portal between the travelling world and the earthly sphere. But while the Whoosh only lasted a second or two, this was going on for minutes. Then, when Aliya was sure part of her was missing – a foot, maybe, or an arm – the carpet slowed and came to a hover. Around her the universe spread out, a mass of darkness and bright stars. Mustafa and Hafiza were nowhere to be seen. She was alone in the vastness of space.

With a surge of panic, she screamed their names, turning this way and that. Then, turning her attention to the carpet, she tried to urge it to find its way back to the others. Could it navigate? And where was the smoke bracelet? Aliya fumbled for Simi, but even she was gone. The terror gave way to tears. For a long time she howled into space, ugly-crying, her nose running. She wiped it carelessly on her sleeve.

When she had exhausted herself, she lay down on her back, the carpet curling around her, as if turning itself into a cradle. It rocked her gently from side to side while she looked up at the stars which, she realized, were grouped into constellations. Surprised, she discerned Karima's face among them.

It was her friend, the way she looked when she was excited, when she was in the middle of telling her something she'd figured out — some new recipe and its cure. Her eyes were alight, like they always got when a new idea caught her, as if she were looking inwards and outwards at once. In those moments, Karima was with you completely, and yet very much absorbed by the marvel in her mind. *She's like Simi*, Aliya thought, surprised at this discovery. *She's my companion, but also something on her own that I can't reach*. There was something about friendship, about loving other people, that did not allow you to hold on too hard, to expect too much.

Now her eyes made out the figure of Geddo, sitting in his armchair, a little bent. His fingers were moving slowly over his rosary, a string of wooden beads he used for prayer, now made up of stars. A new pain bloomed in Aliya's chest and fresh tears rose in her eyes. Geddo had been there always, before she was born. What would the world be without him? The thought of it made her feel unattached, as if floating, just like she actually was doing right now, drifting among the stars. *I can't*, she thought. *It's too hard.* At that moment the carpet began to move and *zip* – they were again flying at the speed of light.

Before she had time to reflect on how unpleasant it was, the insane ride came to a stop and she found herself hovering outside a glimmering door of light that hung in the dark, unattached to anything but sky. Next to her was Hafiza on her carpet, and Mustafa, looking as carpet-sick as she felt. After a panicked fumble, Aliya exhaled in relief. Simi was somehow lodged in her pocket again in key form.

'Didn't you say we wouldn't be able to zip?' Mustafa whimpered. 'Cos that was zipping, right?'

'I suppose I was mistaken,' Hafiza said, looking the children over. 'You both seem to be intact.'

'Wait,' Aliya groaned to the guardian. 'What just happened? I thought I was going to *die*!'

'Me too.' Mustafa shook his head miserably. 'But the ride can't have been more than a second.'

Aliya gestured at the space that stretched out around them.

'I was out there for hours!'

'Yes, well.' Hafiza looked at her curiously. 'Time is a flexible concept. Stargazing is different for everyone. Its duration depends on how much they have to reflect on.'

Stargazing? Aliya stared at her. Had this wacky woman-being sent her into space without warning *on purpose*? She had been convinced that she would die alone, drifting aimlessly through the universe.

'Before you get angry,' Hafiza continued, 'think about what you saw. I'm sure it was important.' Then, before Aliya could say anything else, she clapped her hands together. The doorway in front of them began to open.

'Well, I've brought you to the point in time and space where your guide seems to think you ought to go.'

On the other side of the doorway something green peeked through – a jungle.

'Aren't you coming with us?' Mustafa looked hopefully at Hafiza.

'As I said, I'm the guardian of the in-between. This is as far as I go.'

The children stayed close together as they clambered through the opening.

'Good luck, humans,' Hafiza called after them as the woolly carpets returned to her side. She waved at them once and then, with a *zip*, she and her carpets were gone.

'That was very strange,' Mustafa said, looking back into the starry night. 'Kind of nice, but very strange.'

Aliya nodded, her face grim. All of what she had felt and thought when she was floating under the stars . . . she would have to put it on hold for now. She turned to face the jungle before them.

'That's PLAISTIC,' she said, pointing at a green shrub with waxy leaves. 'This means we're back at the Loopers' headquarters. This is where the locksmiths are.'

Chapter 14
THE HOTHOUSE

For some moments, the friends stood still, gazing around them at sunflowers and oleanders, hibiscus bushes full of yellow and red flowers, and Indian jasmines, their crowns bursting with white blossoms. It would have been beautiful if it had been real, but all the vegetation was made out of PLAISTIC and, as Aliya moved through the greenery, she could feel the flowers train their attention on her, their pistils like eyes, following her movements. She almost expected them to speak, and just like when they had been falling through the space-time glitch, she again felt that she was in *Alice in Wonderland* – in the scene where Alice gets bullied by a garden. A high glass wall indicated they were inside some kind of gigantic hothouse, quite like the dome where the Loopers had held their meeting.

The children followed the smoky arrow as it floated through the artificial greenery. It was speeding up, as if sensing something.

'Maybe we're getting closer,' Aliya called over her shoulder as they followed. 'Maybe this is it.'

They pushed through the thick vegetation, like jungle explorers, weaving through vines and flowering bushes whose leaves grasped at them and whispered. It was humid and stifling, and strangely *void*. All the natural sounds of real nature were missing, Aliya realized, as were the scents. Just like every leaf and bud in this fake jungle, the very air felt alive with some menacing consciousness, as if the whole place was spying on them.

The thought of Geddo came to her again. The pain she had felt when seeing his image in the stars returned, and with it a sense of desperation. How was he? How much time did he have left? She had been through a crazed, mythical city and a magical labyrinth but was still no nearer to finding him a cure, and all the while, Geddo's life was seeping away, like the sand in the hourglass at the try-outs. Mr Kamel, Matron Olfat, even her best friend – all of them thought Geddo was beyond saving. It made no sense that the only one who was giving her any hope was her enemy: Neon Ticker.

Streaks of green light filtered through the plants, hitting her in the face. Pressing forward, the children entered a clearing – a green cave, where a large mound of vegetation took up most of the space.

Then, suddenly, the smoke arrow stilled in midair on top of it. It transformed into a word: *Here*.

'This is it!' Aliya cried. Clawing at the vines, she unearthed a sleeping face. It was Lahza Anwar, one of the senior locksmiths.

She pulled away more foliage to discover more locksmiths, lying in an unconscious heap on the ground, cocooned in a mound of plants. As she desperately tore at the greenery, something caught her by the wrist and pulled her off into the air. After a dizzying tumble, she found herself hanging upside down, her ankle caught in a sturdy dark-green vine. Next, a ficus began slapping its big leaves in her face. Another plant, a lush branch of Bougainvillea, snared itself around her wrist, its small thorns pricking her skin. Mustafa was battling a jasmine bush that had entangled him, its thin branches tightening around his limbs.

After a frantic struggle with the vegetation, they were both hanging upside down, their faces red from the blood collecting in their heads. Aliya wasn't sure if plants could snicker, but around her the jungle seemed to vibrate with some peculiar plant merriment.

'Let's not panic,' Aliya panted. She tried to turn herself around to face Mustafa. When she spoke again, her voice had dropped to a whisper: 'I've got an idea. Last time we visited this crazy place, Aion told me these robots are programmed to respond to commands.'

Mustafa answered with a stifled groan. The jasmine had got a firm hold of his torso and was snaking more green tentacles around his head.

'What if they're just like Dusty, Aion's robot-dog vacuum cleaner? He obeys commands too, but can't multitask. He short-circuited once when we tried to make him sweep and suck at the same time. So, just follow my lead.'

She cleared her throat, then shouted: 'Let's play a game of Simon Says!'

Mustafa's plant had all but submerged him in a cocoon of green leaves and white flowers.

Above them, a multitude of flowerheads bent over to look at Aliya. A snake plant reached out and slapped her on the arm. There was another whisper-like rush through hundreds of leaves.

'Simon says, touch your head,' Aliya called out.

She reached downwards and touched her head. Mustafa tugged an arm free and followed suit, his eyes wide with panic.

'They don't have heads,' Mustafa shout-hissed, nodding up at the flowers.

'Simon says, flap your leaves!' Aliya corrected.

Still nothing.

'Keep trying,' Mustafa urged. 'At least they're listening.'

'Simon says, *flap your leaves*.'

The children began flapping their arms. A ficus next to Mustafa suddenly followed suit, rustling its leaves. An apple tree whipped its branches about so that plastic apples flew in all directions.

'Yes, it's working,' Aliya said. 'You do one!'

'Simon says, wiggle your . . . your . . .' Mustafa cried, looking desperate. He had forgotten the word! The plants went still. 'Pistils! Wiggle your pistils.'

This only partly worked, as only some of the plants had pistils to wiggle, but still – the hothouse was getting on board.

'Tremble your petals!'

'Shake your stems!'

'Wobble your fruits!'

Aliya and Mustafa took turns shouting the commands. Then they began their plan for real.

'Wobble your fruits!' Aliya shouted, while Mustafa cried: 'Wiggle your roots!'

'Sway your stems!' Mustafa cried at the same time as Aliya shouted: 'Bounce your flowers!'

For some moments, it seemed to work. The plants were getting confused, enough for the children to wrest themselves free. Mustafa emerged from his green cocoon, arms waving, flapping fingers and wiggling imaginary branches. Sweat poured down Aliya's brow. The hothouse was hot and humid, like a tropical forest, and here they were carrying on like nursery teachers . . . a plant nursery, in this case. But now the greenery was beginning to lose interest, and was closing in on them again.

They made another desperate attempt to free the locksmiths, with plants snapping and flapping at them and vines trying to trip them and catch their feet. Aliya swatted away the branches that tried to ensnare her, then jumped to free her legs. Standing still was not the best idea in here.

She managed to keep Mustafa free of vegetation long enough for him to examine Lahza.

'I think it's severe time lag,' he said. 'The stage before disintegration begins. They need chronobaric chambers back at the sanatorium, and *fast*.'

Then, there he was. Aliya found him lying on his side, his beard entangled with the moss on the ground, his bald spot greenish in the light.

Professor Nigm. His eyes were closed, as if he were having a peaceful nap. Aliya tore at the vegetation that was cocooning him. *You can't die, not you too*. She tore until her hands were red. Yet even as she stood there, the image of him practising magic fluttered into her mind, and doubt mixed with her relief at finding him. The smoke arrow that had been hovering around Nigm sank down and slipped into one of his pockets. It had reached its goal. Now Aliya had to reach hers.

She pushed herself through the vegetation until she reached a glass wall. Outside was an eerie, blank landscape. It looked like an unfinished painting, where the ground was a beige smudge, and the horizon another uncertain brush stroke across the canvas. They were on the edge of the Infinitum again, where it was coming into being, expanding itself infinitely.

'I'm going to open a portal.' Aliya drew Simi out of her pocket. Her breath caught when she looked down and saw that the nadim had turned even blacker – the vivid metal that made up her key form looked like onyx.

Come on now, she thought, squeezing Simi in her right hand. She felt the Baraka energy beginning to collect. *No more weird detours, just please let this work.* The energy pulsed, heating up her palm, pooling. Now the colours of the Sublimes were radiating from her hand, igniting Simi with an iridescent glow.

She moved along the glass wall until she found a hinged panel that must have been some sort of ventilation window. Sticking the key into the frame, she felt the energy give a pulse, like a beat. Then she pulled the window open.

'You did it!' Mustafa appeared next to her, squeezing her shoulder. 'Look!'

On the other side was a reception with a glossy, white-tiled floor. A genie receptionist sat on a swivel chair behind the desk, casually braiding her purple hair. They could see this because they were right behind her, peeking in through what was probably a filing cabinet.

'Excuse me,' Mustafa said.

The genie went invisible with fright, something that usually happened when their kind were overcome by strong emotions.

'We didn't mean to startle you,' Mustafa continued, 'but we really need your help. We've got the locksmiths here and—'

'Opening portals inside the reception area is strictly forbidden!' the genie shrieked. A spray of spit hit Aliya in the face.

'But this is an emergency—' she tried.

'Then you should have used the emergency portal located in the left wing of the sanatorium!'

The genie's face appeared again and she glared at them through the portal. But as she did, she caught sight of the collapsed Janus Quartz on the ground behind them, cocooned in greenery.

'Oh dear, oh dear!' she cried, disappearing again. Aliya watched the handset of an intercom float into the air, before she had to fight off another load of the green tendrils attempting to ensnare her.

'Attention all nurses!' the genie cried. 'Report to reception immediately. We have a situation. I repeat: we have a situation.'

Chapter 15
THE MIRACLE CURE

Aliya had just helped a dazed Professor Nigm through the portal into the sanatorium when the voice rang out behind her – a voice so familiar that she could have been in the Smithy on a Monday morning, not here in this fake garden, bundling her mentor through an unauthorized portal. At the voice's command, the PLAISTIC plants shrank back obediently and became still.

It was Arsinoe who stood there, dressed like a Looper in a white cloak and hood that hung off her shoulders. Her honey-coloured hair was as glossy as ever, as though nothing about her had changed. She was the same stylish senior, looking down at Aliya with her usual condescending gaze. Her chameleon nadim sat on her shoulder, no longer black, but glowing with a metallic sheen that reflected the greens of the hothouse – so bright he almost looked unreal. What had happened to him?

Aliya felt for Simi, in bird form, who was perched on her shoulder, so dark now she looked like a blackbird.

'The locksmiths can go,' Arsinoe said. 'And your friend too. We don't need them. I'm afraid they won't be much use to anyone any more.'

'What do you mean?' Aliya frowned. 'What have you done to them?'

'Not me,' Arsinoe said. 'It was spending time in the future that did it. Neon stowed them away for just long enough to reach this stage of time lag. Then he brought them back here, to trap you. Neon knew you would come looking for your mentor, that you'd gate-crash the Great Race. Quite a simple plan, really.'

Aliya shook her head, outraged.

'But they're your friends. Our teachers!'

Glancing behind her, she saw faces staring back at her through the portal. Nurses, the genie secretary, security personnel.

'Come on, Aliya!' Mustafa had already made it to the other side and was there too, waving at her. Aliya took a step towards him and safety, but the portal closed suddenly. Turning, Aliya saw that Arsinoe was aiming a metal stick at it. It was a wand, an actual wand, like something from *Harry Potter*. She was still wearing the leather gloves, the same ones she'd pulled on in the Smithy the morning of the try-outs. Had that only been just a few days ago?

'You're a traitor,' Aliya said after a moment of silence.

Arsinoe winced a little at the word. It was the worst thing possible, to break the locksmith code, the travel code. It had been drilled into them. The travel world was a refuge, a sacred place built on mutual understanding and trust. It could only continue to exist if they all kept it safe and secret. But Arsinoe had thrown that away as though it meant nothing.

'This is bigger than you and me,' the senior said at last. 'You've got to play along if you want to live.'

'Is that what you're doing? *Playing along*?' Aliya's mouth was suddenly so dry it felt difficult to form words. 'Because you're afraid of them? The Loopers?'

'I'm being smart,' Arsinoe said.

'Breaking the locksmith code is smart?'

Arsinoe gave a mirthless laugh. 'I lost my powers when *he* possessed me. It ruptured the bond between my nadim and me, and . . . I'm not a locksmith any more.'

'But you spent all that time in the sanatorium. I thought—'

'You thought wrong.'

That summer, on board the *Silver Express*, Dorian had possessed Arsinoe. He had intended to use her to get into the Smithy, to reach the Sublimes and execute his plan, but things hadn't played out the way he had intended. Proteus, Arsinoe's nadim, had turned black and she had lost her powers. Aliya knew all that, she had been there, but she hadn't imagined it was a permanent change. She'd realized, like everyone at the Smithy had, that Arsinoe and Proteus's recovery was a slow process, but she'd assumed they would eventually be restored to normal, or at least something close to it. Arsinoe had certainly acted as though that were the case.

Despite occasionally showing glimpses of discomfort and vulnerability, she'd been attending classes at the Smithy and treating everyone in her usual pleasant but slightly patronizing manner.

'Was that why you made me open the portal when we were going home the other day?' Aliya asked. 'You pretended you were supervising my practice, but really you couldn't do it yourself?'

'If I could access the Smithy, there would be no need for you. But I've spent the whole semester following others in and out. It's *you* the Loopers need. You're the hero of the hour.'

The sarcasm of her last remark was evident, but she also sounded jealous. Though who could envy someone who had been made a pawn in the destruction of a whole world?

'Why?' Aliya said. 'Did they promise you your powers back? If you do their bidding?'

Arsinoe smiled.

'I'm learning magic, of course. But it's more than that. I *belong* with the elite, Aliya. It's just who I am. It sounds terrible, I know, but some people are just . . .' She made a gesture in the air with the hand that wasn't holding the wand.

'Better than everyone else?' Aliya frowned. 'So, you deserve to live on in some perfect bubble for ever while the rest of us are destroyed?'

'It doesn't have to be like that. You could apply and see what happens.'

'You mean I could come along as a slave?'

'On second thoughts, I'm not sure you would qualify. You're too . . . spirited. But perhaps after they trained you.'

'Tortured me, you mean?'

Aliya remembered the glowing armbands she had seen on the mythicals serving at the Loopers' meeting. Metaphysical bonds that would turn them to ash if they rebelled.

'It's only torture if you resist. Oh, Aliya, you're taking such a bleak view of this. I actually came to offer you the opportunity of a lifetime.'

'What?' Aliya felt her cheeks heating up. She despaired at Arsinoe's incomprehensible deceit, at her belief that some people were better and more worthy than others . . . worthy of living, while others were dispensable. 'I'm never bargaining with that demon again. You can't tempt me or promise me *anything* that would make me choose magic, ever. Get it?'

'I see.' Arsinoe rolled the wand between her gloved fingers. 'But what if it wasn't *you* we promised something to? What if it was someone else?'

Aliya stared at her.

'You mean my friends? Where are they?'

'They were rounded up in the hall of mirrors. They will be kept in safe storage with the rest of the Sweepers and race pods until the Loop is completed. Then things will . . . take their natural course. As we speak, the sanatorium is being surrounded by our allies. The locksmiths will be seized and executed for treason tomorrow morning in Qahira Square. The whole Citadel believes they are the conspirators causing the cracks in the atmosphere – or at least the ones who matter do. It's a marvel what you can accomplish with threats, some well-aimed media coverage and generous bribes.'

She paused to push a wayward tendril of golden hair back in place. 'Tonight, we will give the locksmiths a chance to consider which side they want to be on. They'll have to be blotted, of course, or we would never be able to trust them in the Loop. But there are some individuals of quality among them. That can't be denied. You'll be pleased to know that your mentor is among the ones being considered. He even has some experience of magic already, doesn't he? Oh, how the mighty have fallen.' She smiled. 'But back to the matter in hand – I wasn't talking about your friends, Aliya. I was talking about someone even closer to you. Your grandfather.'

Aliya felt a rush of cold panic.

'What have you done to him?'

'That's what I've been meaning to tell you. The elect are giving you a chance to save him.'

She searched in the fold of her dress and brought out a vial made of blue glass.

'We've got the antidote, you see, to the poison that's killing your grandfather. We'll let you have it, but first you've got to do something for us. Something that should be so easy for a locksmith of your calibre.' She pronounced the last word as though it tasted bad. 'You have to let us into the Smithy, that's all.'

They stood for some moments, looking at each

other. Aliya couldn't believe she'd been with this girl just days before, thinking about how they'd both had a narrow escape from Dorian aboard the *Silver Express*, that the worst was behind them. She had felt sorry for Arsinoe.

'What happened to you the other day in the Smithy?' Aliya asked, nodding at Arsinoe's gloved hands. It was a question, but she'd already half-guessed the answer. 'The Sublimes burnt you, didn't they?'

'All I did was ask them to give me my powers back. But they did this to me.' She pulled off a glove and showed Aliya her blackened hand, nails like fragments of coal. 'You thought they'd be more forgiving, for all their *sublimity*.' She scoffed. 'But they rejected me. That's when I made up my mind. I'll go somewhere where I'm wanted. Neon had spoken to me several times before about joining the Loopers. Said I belonged with them.'

'Did they . . . sense something in you? The Sublimes?' Aliya's heart was thumping, her throat cramping. She felt the weight of Simi on her shoulder. The blackness on Arsinoe's hands was a sign –

the mark of a curse, of an exile. And Aliya had it too. Her nadim had it.

'Come on,' Arsinoe said, ignoring her question. 'We're expected.'

After a short ride in a whizzcalator over the lush, artificial landscape, Arsinoe and Aliya arrived at a gigantic, egg-shaped building – Neon's signature style. As she passed through the arched entrance, Aliya realized that what she had thought was white marble was actually screens. The whole building – every inch of it – was covered in sleek, electronic slabs that *displayed* marble. The floor too displayed a thick-piled blue carpet.

'Welcome!'

Aliya jumped in fright as every screen around her, from the floor to the high vaulted ceiling, suddenly showed the face of Neon Ticker. He was everywhere, with pink hair, looking straight at her – a perfect smile projected a thousand-fold. As Aliya followed Arsinoe deeper into this digital cathedral, the scene shifted again, to display a beach, then a bustling market, then a quiet meadow where the wind whispered through the grass.

As Arsinoe and Aliya stopped at the centre, the screens returned to marble. At the far end a splendid chair was rising out of the floor, like something from a popstar's stage show. Its back was towards them, and as it began to turn, it sparkled so much that Aliya had to squint. Neon was sitting on the throne, dressed in a silvery robe. He looked like an ancient king turned DJ.

'What do you think of my cathedral?' Neon smiled up at the expanse of the ceiling. 'A thing of beauty, isn't she? And not just *one* thing! With the press of a button, this space can turn into almost anything you wish for.'

'It was you, wasn't it?!' Aliya spat. 'Ever since the first time, in the Smithy, and then at the try-outs. You booby-trapped the race to suck us into the Shop!'

Neon peered down at Aliya with a frown – a ruler displeased with an uncouth visitor, with this child who dared shout in his cathedral.

'Aren't we abrupt,' he said, then thought for a moment. 'Well, the race, yes, that was us. I also opened a portal to the Shop at the try-outs, hoping to capture you. But at the Smithy? No, my dear, that wasn't me.' Tilting his head, he studied her. 'How interesting. A locksmith who opens portals to the Shop of Second Chances all on her own, and from *within* the Smithy. What's going on there, I wonder? Just think of the scandal if *that* got out.'

'I didn't!' Aliya shouted. 'You're lying.'

Neon frowned as though her voice hurt his ears.

'I know all this must be a shock for you. But we're not asking much. In fact, as I think our sister Arsinoe here has explained, we're offering you a great blessing in exchange for a small service.'

'Where is my grandfather?'

Neon stood up. 'If you would follow me.'

An elevator took them down into the bowels of the cathedral and there, in a brightly lit room set up like an operating theatre, Geddo lay on a table, as white as a sheet. A group of mythical orderlies in white scrubs moved away to let them through. Aliya threw herself on her grandfather and began looking him over.

'The poison has left him very weak,' Neon said.

'This is your chance. Give him the antidote.' He took the glass vial from Arsinoe and held it up. 'A few drops are all it takes.'

Aliya stood up, facing him.

'I can't open the Smithy,' she said.

'Whyever not?' Neon said. He was smiling, but there was nothing kind in his eyes.

'Because it means the end of the travel world.'

Neon hooted and boxed the air.

'It means the beginning of a *new* world, you silly little girl! A world free of strife and problems and worries . . . of imperfections and *death*! So, yes, perhaps it means the end of this ugly travel world that you're so fond of, but there's always a price to pay for something great. Look' – Neon wrung his hands – 'I'll give you a chance to join our movement once you've done your part, all right? You and your grandfather. There!' As he tapped a device on his wrist, a holographic image appeared in the air between them – a radiant bracelet, just like the ones she had seen the mythicals wearing at the Loopers' meeting. Jewellery that really was metaphysical bond that would maim or strangle their victims, and eventually turn them to dust if they resisted the commands of their masters.

'We've got many varieties if you don't like this one,' Neon said. Swiping the image, another bracelet appeared, equally radiant. 'There are necklaces too.' Neon gave her a wry smile. 'But maybe not?'

Aliya took a step back, remembering the necklace Dorian had once used to capture and almost kill her. Neon, of course, knew her history with magic necklaces.

'Now, I hate to be firm,' he went on. 'I like to be the good guy, you know, but you really are being very stubborn. But, oh! I know who might change your mind. We've got a friend of yours here. We rescued her from the hall of mirrors and offered her a chance to join us. Call her in, will you?' Neon waved at one of the mythical orderlies. 'Now, look over there.'

Aliya turned in the direction Neon was pointing. For a moment she thought her heart would stop beating. In the doorway, dressed in the same white cloak as Arsinoe, was Victoria.

'Victoria?' Aliya stumbled over to her friend.

'What's going on?' Reaching her, Aliya grabbed her friend by the sleeve. 'Why are you dressed like that? How did you even get here—'

Victoria pushed her aside as she made her way into the room. Aliya followed, confused.

'What are you doing?' Aliya asked. Then, lowering her voice to a whisper: 'Are you undercover? Is this because they threatened to kill you?' Of course her friend was just playing along to buy time.

Victoria gave her a stern look.

'You want an explanation,' she said. 'Fair enough. I know this is hard for you to understand . . . but then they gave me a very hard choice.' Victoria looked at her white slippers. 'I'd rather be a Looper than dead . . . or a slave. That was the other option. Do you see?'

Aliya shook her head. *No, no, no.* This wasn't real. This couldn't be happening.

Victoria turned and started to walk away. Aliya grabbed her by the arm of her white cloak.

'We'll think of some way to get out of this,' Aliya whispered desperately. 'You won't have to go through with it. You can't join *them*.'

'Be smart for once in your life, Aliya.' Victoria squeezed her hand. There were tears in her eyes. 'Make the trade and save your grandfather's life. Choose to do this the easy way. They're going to make you open the Smithy whether you want to or not. Don't you understand that? At least if you comply, you'll save some lives. Don't be heroic like those old duffers in the Brigade. Heroism is really just selfish at this point.'

Aliya stared at her. How could she say this? This couldn't be real. She closed her eyes. Maybe, if she wanted it hard enough, it would all go away. They would be safe again, back in their common room sitting in front of the fire, eating Mrs Dickens's caramel popcorn.

'Frankly,' Neon said behind them, 'I'm already late for a meeting. I'm giving you thirty seconds to agree, or it's bye-bye, Grandpa.'

Turning, Aliya saw that an orderly was readying a big syringe.

'No,' Aliya said. She gave Victoria a last look. 'Don't touch him. I'll do what you want.'

Chapter 16
QAHIRA SQUARE

Was sacrificing the whole world justified if it was for someone you loved? For someone you couldn't imagine existing without? Or was it selfish?

Those were the thoughts that swirled around in Aliya's head like an ominous flock of crows the next morning, just before sunrise, as she and the rest of Neon's gang gathered at Qahira Square. Neon was elated, jumping up and down and this way and that, rubbing his hands, looking at the golden door that would soon open and admit him to the Smithy. But not quite yet.

The morning had brought a cold mist that filled the square, creeping up the walls of the departments, submerging the eateries and stalls. Apart from

Neon's excited chatter, the square was still. An eerie quiet reigned, all the more oppressive because of the large crowd of Loopers who had assembled. Their faces hidden by their hoods, they had all turned towards the stage that had been erected a few paces away from the Smithy's door. Somewhere in the sea of white cloaks, Aliya knew, were Arsinoe and Victoria. And Dorian, where was he? Aliya looked around anxiously. She hadn't seen him since the Loopers' meeting. Somehow, not knowing where he was and when he would show up was even more chilling than seeing him.

On the stage sat a futuristic contraption, its grey metal dull in the faint light – a doorway made of steel, except for the neon blade that blazed and vibrated on top of the rectangular form.

'Behold the guillotine of the future!' Neon called out, addressing the windows of the surrounding buildings, where Aliya could see faces looking down at them. No one who wasn't a Looper had come out. She wasn't sure if what Arsinoe had told her was true: that the city still believed in the guilt of the locksmiths. But if they did, wouldn't they be out here, cheering? Turning, she spotted the face of a woman peering through a nearby window. It was Hannah, who worked at the rare books shop near Pastroudis Sweets. On a floor above her, Aliya saw Abu Bakr from the dry-cleaners near the hostel, and Girgis, from Fuad's favourite coffee shop. The fear in their eyes told Aliya everything she needed to know. The city didn't want the Loopers. They had recognized them for what they were – a gang of entitled sociopaths.

'I got the idea when I visited the French Revolution.' Neon turned to Aliya. 'Have you been? Such an exciting time.' When she said nothing, he went on. 'It's the efficiency, you see.' He pointed at the blade – the only radiant thing in the gloom. It pulsed and shuddered, shifting in colour from bright yellow to stark pink. 'The laser beam cuts the head clean off, but without the mess. It cauterizes the wound as it cuts.' Neon did a chopping movement with his hand. 'They won't feel a thing, plus there's minimal mess.'

Aliya met Neon's eyes. His hair was still pink, with some added silver streaks. Up close his face looked strangely plastic, as though he had forgotten to peel off some kind of face mask. But maybe that was it – maybe Neon was more plastic than human. This was the reason he could look like an excited schoolboy as he moved around the stage where the soon-to-be victims of his futuristic killing machine stood, huddled together, their hands bound behind their backs.

Only an hour ago, Aliya had been obliged to leave Geddo, cold and barely breathing, on that table in the bowels of Neon's cathedral. As soon as this was over, Neon had promised, she would get the antidote and be able to save him. Now, her eyes burnt as she recognized the adults lined up for execution. There was Madame Hippolyta in a simple sackcloth shift, stripped of her ornaments – her pearls and crystals and feathers – like a plucked bird. Behind her stood Mr Kamel, looking skywards. Aliya could see the glowing bonds that tied his ankles together, just like the ones the rest of the Night Folk alongside him were wearing. Simple ropes wouldn't work to bind the likes of them.

Aliya recognized the greasy-haired sphinx,

Magda, and many of the other mythicals she had met at the Grizzled Hen. They too must have been captured in the racecourse or rounded up afterwards. Huddling on the ground behind them, still too woozy to stand up, were the locksmiths. Aliya felt herself go cold all over again as she recognized Omar Sadik, her fellow locksmith apprentice. Behind him Janus Quartz sat on a stool. Professor Nigm was sitting up straight with closed eyes. How had it come to this? Only a week ago she had been walking next to him in the bright corridors of the Smithy, dreaming about the future, of possibilities. Aliya wished he would look at her. But then, remembering her part in the orchestration of these events, she instead wished she could sink through the ground and disappear.

'Let's begin!' Neon clapped his hands together. 'Let the traitors taste our justice!'

Two Loopers grabbed hold of Madame Hippolyta and tugged her towards the guillotine. She resisted. Then, recognizing someone in the crowd, she shouted, 'You, Harold. I see you! And you, Leander . . . Don't think those capes can hide you. *Everyone* here knows what you are. What you and your friends are. You're nothing but thugs. Cowardly thugs!'

Behind Hippolyta, the mythicals began struggling against their bonds, the ghouls raising their voices in fierce cries. The sila from the Grizzled Hen was wearing her thundercloud wrapped around her shoulders like a cape. As she screamed, a single, limp lightning bolt shot into the sky, cutting the mist. The magic of her bonds, Aliya knew, was reining it in. It didn't stop the rain, though, which began drizzling over the stage.

As the Loopers secured Hippolyta's head to the guillotine's block, an odd sound sliced through the mist. It was a whistle. A singular, high, piercing sound. A silence followed, and then . . . the sound of feet – a fast, rhythmic marching coming closer.

Turning, Aliya saw them coming – emerging out of the side streets and alleys, like a tsunami of grey metal.

Security robots. They were coming from all sides, surrounding the square, filling each alley and side street, their footfalls uniform, their black visors down. Each metallic hand was grasping a baton.

Two short whistles rang out, and the robots stopped with a rhythmic *click-clack*.

Someone was approaching on a flying carpet. At first, only the underside was visible, but as it sank and came to a hover above the first line of robots, directly opposite the stage, Aliya saw Inspector Prickly standing, broad-legged, a whistle between his teeth.

Next to him – Aliya's heart somersaulted – was Victoria, holding a megaphone and staring defiantly down at the Loopers.

If Aliya had possessed wings, she would have flown up and caught her friend – not a Looper! – in a joyous hug. She suddenly realized how this had come about: Victoria had told her how she had been helping her father control the robots, and now they were clearly obeying every command of his whistle.

After a nod from her father, Victoria raised the megaphone to her lips.

'Listen up, cowardly scum!' she shouted. 'You are completely surrounded. If you want your mummies to recognize you, I suggest you come along peaceably when the robots move in to make arrests.'

Inspector Prickly blew another burst through the whistle. Slowly, the robots advanced on the Loopers, who were beginning to panic and push, looking for ways to escape.

Aliya, who had been hooting jubilantly, choked as a large hand grabbed her around the throat.

'Now listen, girl,' a voice hissed into her ear – the same voice that haunted her nightmares. 'You open the door to the Smithy,' Dorian Darke said, 'or I'll snap your little neck in two.'

He squeezed. Aliya's vision blurred, the world around her turning into fragments, like a puzzle coming apart. There was no air, just the relentless pressure of Dorian's metallic fingers digging into her flesh, closing her windpipe. Then Simi was in her hands, already in key form, pulsing with energy. She'd lit up on her own, as if she wanted to be used.

Open the door.

The words pulsed soundlessly through her heart and at once Aliya knew: this was Simi's voice speaking to her.

Open it. It will be all right. I promise.

Chapter 17
A DEADLY EMBRACE

Magic surrounded her like a forest fire. The barrier Dorian had raised flickered between Prickly's robots and the Loopers, who were now pushing past her into the Smithy. Aliya stood trembling in the golden doorway, sweat seeping down her brow. It was too late. She had done it. She had opened the Smithy and saved her neck, quite literally. Dorian had not let his stranglehold go until the door had opened. Then, he had pushed her aside like something worthless and made his way inside.

She felt sick. Raising a hand to her throat, she swallowed, willing the nausea to subside. She would have to find Neon, demand the antidote, or all of this would have been in vain. The relentless feeling of having made the wrong choice overcame her again, and this time she couldn't hold back. Leaning over, she threw up on the stony ground next to the Smithy's entrance.

It had taken Dorian seconds to create the magical barrier that kept Inspector Prickly and his robots at bay. On the other side, a multitude of metal faces stared back at her – the police robots, waiting for a new command. But what command could Prickly give to stop magic?

Turning, she walked into the Smithy, leaving the portal open behind her. What did it matter now, who entered and who left? The travel world had already been given its death blow. But would it be a quick death? Or slow and agonizing?

Moving through the Smithy, she followed the trail of destruction the Loopers had left in their wake: hieracosphinxes lay collapsed – dead or stunned, she did not know. Broken glass from smashed cabinets and torn-down instruments were strewn across her path as she made her way deeper into the maze of corridors. Would the Smithy defend itself by shifting its walls around the Loopers?

But Dorian had been elder locksmith here, and probably still knew the place like the back of his hand. It wasn't a place you forgot. He would probably use magic to force it to comply.

Dazed, Aliya stopped at a corner and caught herself. Where was she going? Why was she following them? She needed the antidote that Neon had promised her, yes, but also . . . where else could she go? In a single moment, she had become an outcast – the one who opened the Smithy to the enemy, who broke the locksmith code and enabled the travel world's destruction. As if in response to her thought, the ground rumbled under her. An earthquake. The world was writhing in distress.

As she moved deeper into the building, the hum grew in intensity, reaching her through the ground, the walls. The very air was filled with it, until it seemed as though it was part of her too, echoing through the cavities in her heart, beating through her blood.

The Sublimes, she thought. She whispered their name over and over, like a mantra, until she arrived at the silver door, at the mouth of the cave which was the Sublimes' dwelling place and the centre of the travel world – where it had begun and where it would now end. Why had Simi told her to open the door? How could any of this ever be OK again?

The Loopers had filled the cave, their white cloaks dappled in the colours of the magnificent Baraka energy: silvers, pinks and blues danced across the white textile, making the intruders look benign, not like the parasites they really were.

Neon and Dorian were standing on the balcony that overlooked the pit where the Sublimes lived. They too were bathed in the glorious light that emanated from below – Neon with his white robes and silver-streaked hair, Dorian in his strange AI body.

Now, Dorian drew his key out and held it over his head, triumphant. Aliya saw the Darkling's head, growing in size even as Dorian held it, the blind cavity where its eye should have been gaping at her.

'With this,' he began, 'our magic will be invincible. With this, we will raze the old world to the ground and build a new one!'

They wouldn't let him go through with it. Aliya

remembered how the Sublimes had burnt Arsinoe's hands and desperately hoped the same would happen now. *They'll repel him!*

A shudder went through the ground, and the Sublimes' hum grew in volume. Now the Darkling was transforming, filling the cave with its expanding, scaly black body. The Loopers pushed back out into the corridor in alarm, carrying Aliya with them. The snake's body kept coming, uncoiling as it grew until its tail end was pushing its way through the corridors towards the exit. Aliya, pressed against a corridor wall, watched as the snake body became so thick she wouldn't be able to wrap her arms around it. She stood, frozen, staring at it, unable to move or think. And then Dorian pushed past her, shoving her out of his way. She had performed her task and was unimportant now. Not even important enough to kill.

She followed him as he swept out through the golden door and into Qahira Square, where the Darkling's tail tip was writhing on the stony ground, its body pulsing with light. The black scales were lit from within. It was channelling Sublime energy. *Why had the Sublimes let it?* The Darkling was fulfilling its mission. It had never just been a travel key. Dorian had crafted it out of something else, back when her mother had still been alive – an ouroboros – an artefact used to transform magic into good energy. But now he was making it do the reverse.

Had her mother been aware of Dorian's plans? Had she known what he intended to do with the key she had helped him create when she was his apprentice all those years ago?

The magic was still holding off the security robots. In the square next to the Smithy's golden door, Dorian had stopped, his outstretched arms jubilant in victory.

Aliya felt another tremor and the ground shifted beneath her feet. From the other side of the magical barrier came a cry, and then a deep rift opened in the sky above them, stretching like a giant claw mark across the square from one side to the other.

Dorian was looking up into the torn sky, mumbling something.

'He's calling it,' a voice said next to Aliya. 'The

Shop.' It was Arsinoe. Her hood had fallen off her head. 'Stay with me.' She took Aliya's hand. 'I'll let you work for me. I'll take care of you. For old times' sake.'

'Be your slave, you mean?'

Was the senior imagining that she was doing her a favour? That this was kindness in the midst of a crumbling world?

'Why did you do it?' Aliya asked. A new shudder went through the ground, rumbling against the soles of her feet.

'He gave me a taste of magic, and . . . I couldn't go back. It's addictive, like a drug. Oh, look!' Arsinoe pointed. 'It's happening.'

It began as a doorway – a mirror image of the Smithy's golden one that materialized right in front of it. Then black bricks began to appear, building around the doorway, stone by stone, until there stood a shop, complete with a grimy display window and a dirt-brown awning. It was the Shop of Second Chances.

Now the door opened, like a mouth in the brickwork. Energy from the Darkling's tail began seeping through it, feeding it.

'It's working!' Arsinoe shrieked, clapping her hands.

Aliya stood frozen, watching as the Shop transformed. It was not just growing in size, but developing turrets, towers. New windows were popping up among the brickwork. The Shop was a beast made of bricks with windows for eyes and towers for horns. The original doorway grew too, into a wide grin of a portal, with spiked wrought-iron bars for teeth.

The magical barrier pushed forward, pressing the robots back into the side streets and alleys, until the whole square was occupied by magic, with the Shop towering over the departments – a huge, black castle.

Aliya felt another rumble and yet another rift tore the sky. Blackness stared out at her, a void of nothingness. Now, streaming through the Shop's gaping jaws, came cursed items: walking hat stands; porcelain figurines magically swelled to the size of grown men; cursed teapots, a crowd of teacups dancing after them like ducklings after their mother;

old, rusty weapons swinging through the air; leather boots walking on their own. The Shop was spilling its innards into the square, a menagerie of wicked paraphernalia – a scene that would have been comical had there not been so much evil pulsing through it.

Aliya was knocked into the golden doorframe as Neon Ticker pushed past her. He ran up to Dorian, like an excited schoolboy to his favourite teacher.

'What are we waiting for?' he panted. 'Is the magic strong enough?'

Dorian turned his handsome, artificial face to him. It was hard to read his expression, seeing that he no longer had skin or muscles.

'It's time to do what I've been waiting for my whole life as an exile.' Dorian's voice was strangely toneless, despite the weight of his words. 'The reason I chose magic and learnt its ways, why I was shunned and exiled from everything, even my own body.' He gestured down at the machine Neon had built him.

As he stepped into the doorway of the Shop, Aliya saw his lips moving with new incantations.

Energy was still streaming through the Darkling's tail into the Shop, its castle-body expanding all the while. There was a constant clatter of new bricks piling up, the pop and crack of new windows appearing. The building had begun to look almost like a spider, with its large black body and multiple eyes.

A surge of magic burst out of the Shop and hit Dorian in the chest, snaking around him in flame-coloured swathes. It seeped into him, through his hands, his back, his head, until his eyes began to glow like red-hot pokers. Dorian roared – whether in pain or triumph, Aliya didn't know. His voice rose as he spat out spells, chanting, his hands stretched out before him. The magic intensified, building into a firestorm. Aliya took a step into the open doorway, squeezing next to the Darkling's tail, shielding her face with her arm.

Then, suddenly, Dorian Darke was looking at her.

'See,' he called, gesturing at himself, at his artificial body, his burning eyes. 'See what I did for love? What I sacrificed?'

His voice was full of angry triumph. It was as though he was cursing her and bragging, all at once.

'And you...' He pointed at her with his glowing hand. 'You're just like me.'

Through the flowing light, so strong it made her eyes tear, Aliya could see the ground in front of Dorian begin to break open. The cobblestones crumbled, and out of the pit a figure ascended. As she rose, the magic sank to the ground and came to a simmer around her and Dorian's feet, like a ring of fire. The figure was coming from the innards of the earth, yet she looked as if she had descended from the sky, all clean and fresh, her hair flowing down her shoulders. The ground closed beneath her bare feet. Behind Dorian, Neon scrambled into the Shop for cover. Arsinoe pressed herself past Aliya into the Smithy.

Dorian had stopped chanting and was staring at the figure. Her back was to Aliya, but she knew who it was. She had seen her before. This was his older sister, who had given her life to protect him.

'Cassandra,' Dorian croaked, taking a wobbly step towards her. 'You are back, at last. I-I did it. I raised you from the dead.'

For some moments, all was still. Cassandra stood

calmly regarding Dorian. Above them, the Shop's windows stared down at them like large, black eyes.

'Come to me, brother,' the figure said, stretching her arms out. 'Come and embrace me.'

Dorian quickly moved forward and fell into her arms.

Aliya held her breath. This was the fulfilment of Dorian's dream. This was why *her* mother and father had died – so that Dorian could access magic strong enough to defy Death itself. All to get his sister back. How, then, could he have claimed that Aliya was anything like him?

Now, a large, awkward figure appeared in the entrance to the shop – a scarecrow made of items piled together. It moved clunkily forward until it stood next to the embracing pair, just outside the burning ring of magic. Its head was a lampshade, its throat a wooden recorder. It had eyes made of marbles and lips made of hair clips and drawing pins. A heap of inanimate things, yet, through the mechanics of magic, it had a face and a mouth that opened and spoke, in a voice filtered through the recorder, high-pitched and eerie.

'Such a long-time student of magic, and after so much sacrifice . . . still you refuse to acknowledge our limits. How very human.' The thing shook its head, making the beaded edge of its lampshade head chime. 'Magic can give you the world, fulfil your wishes, grant your desires, but you of all people should've known what it *cannot* do. It is powerless to move time, give you love or bring back what has died.'

The figure sighed, and Aliya realized that this was the Shop itself speaking.

'You can never master a thing if you ignore its limits and your own,' it continued. 'What you are holding in your arms is not your sister, but a demon come from hell to bring you to your final destination. Your sister's soul is protected in a place neither of us could ever reach.'

The Shop gestured skyward with a hand made of chopsticks and an old doll's head. Turning, it hobbled back through the gates of its castle. Now that the truth was out, the demon shed its disguise and appeared in its true form. The soft flesh of Cassandra's arms turned to fire. Her hair dissolved and a black scalp appeared, above a skeletal face with eyes like burning coals. Dorian roared, struggling frantically in the demon's grasp, his artificial body melting as the demon squeezed. Beneath them, the ground was opening once more. The demon tumbled backwards, and they both fell into the burning darkness. The last thing Aliya heard was Dorian's hoarse scream. Then the ground closed again, leaving no trace behind.

Chapter 18
A POCKET IN TIME

Aliya stared at the ground where Dorian had disappeared. Next to her, Arsinoe was screaming incoherently. The world moved past Aliya as if she were underwater, distant and slow. She saw Neon, wild-eyed, staring around him. Following his gaze, she realized that it wasn't Dorian's disappearance he was concerned about.

Something was happening with the Darkling. Right next to Aliya's feet, the tail still lay pulsing, but also twitching. She jumped out of the way, just as it came crashing into the doorframe.

Aliya felt Simi struggling in her pocket. The nadim had transformed from key to bird again. Now she wriggled free, gave Aliya a reproachful look and, hopping on to her hand, ruffled her iridescent feathers. Aliya stared. Simi was as black as a crow! She matched the Darkling's tail, as if she'd become an extension of the snake.

'Go on,' she cried at the nadim. 'Save yourself! Fly!'

With a screech, Simi hurled herself into the sky, leaving Aliya staring after her. Her nadim had been trapped too long, held back from whatever it was she wanted, and now – what would happen? What would she do? Aliya stood watching the bird as she swooped up and disappeared behind one of the Shop's turrets. It was like watching her own blackened heart fly away from her, escaping.

'The Darkling is breaking free!' Neon yelled at Arsinoe, gesturing at the whipping tail. 'We've got to control it!'

'I'm not touching that.' Arsinoe, wide-eyed with horror, was backing away. 'That's pure Sublime energy! I'll get burnt alive!'

'You swore!' Neon reached out and grabbed the fleeing girl by the hair. 'You swore to help build the new world. There's no turning back now. I command you!'

'I'm not one of your slaves!' Arsinoe shrieked, turning in his grasp to face him. 'You can't tell me what to do!'

'Oh, yes, I can,' Neon shouted, spit flying. 'You're all slaves, every one of you! Every single one of you—'

He howled as Arsinoe bit his hand. For a moment, he looked as though he would chase her as she fled, but as the tail end of the Darkling whipped past him, he grabbed hold of it.

'Obey me!' he shouted. There was a pause before his eyes popped in horrified surprise. For a moment they met Aliya's where she stood by the golden door. She yelped in shock as his face lit up from within like a bulb. His pink hair lifted off his radiant face and stood on end and he twitched helplessly, like a frantic marionette. In a flash, his body lit up, sparks flying around him – a human sparkler.

The shock of seeing Dorian disappear had frozen Aliya to the spot, but now something set her in motion. She had to save this horrible man, if only because he had her grandfather's antidote. The glass bottle he had shown her back in the underbelly of his cathedral – she needed it. It was the sole reason she had betrayed everyone and opened the Smithy.

Moving quickly, she reached Neon and tugged at the hand with which he had gripped the Darkling's tail. It did not work. The hand was frozen, attached to the tail with a cramped grip. What would happen if *she* touched the snake? Neon stared at her, his eyes popping, froth building at the corners of his mouth. He would die in moments unless she intervened.

Closing her eyes, she concentrated, then felt her power pool into her palms. She carefully touched the black scales and bent Neon's cramped fingers loose. Her touch sent a visible shiver through the snake's tail. Finally free, Neon fell backwards, the hand that had clutched the tail charred and black. He lay gaping on his back, staring at the sky. Aliya poked him with her foot. Was he dead? Leaning in closer, she heard his ragged breath.

Moments passed as Aliya crouched next to Neon, waiting for him to recover enough to speak to her. Around them, the magical barrier flashed like fire.

'The antidote,' she said finally, leaning over him. 'Please, my grandfather doesn't have long.'

Neon weakly nodded downwards, and Aliya searched the pockets of his tunic until she found it – the blue glass vial. But lifting it, she sensed it was too light. She tipped it over and realized why. It was empty.

'No!' Aliya stood up, staring from the empty bottle to Neon. 'No, no, no!' She threw the bottle on the ground next to him and it smashed to pieces. Neon coughed and some blood seeped out of his mouth. He looked up at her, grimacing.

'My promises have never been worth much.'

Now an army of cursed items clattered in around him and carried him away. He disappeared into the Shop, carried as if on a stretcher atop the cursed paraphernalia. He would be made to live in it, Aliya guessed, just like the teapots and hat stands. His soul would be harvested to feed the magic. Perhaps he would be made to replace Dorian as shopkeeper?

Behind her, the golden doorway of the Smithy quaked. As she turned, Aliya saw the Darkling's blind head coming towards her down the long corridor, its forked tongue like a cracking whip.

The ground underneath her shook. The world

trembled, as if it knew it was falling to pieces. Aliya looked around. She was trapped. Behind her was the Shop, its doorway gaping at her like a toothless mouth. She could feel the magic pulsing out of it, sucking at her, stirring up a strange feeling in her chest, like the one she sometimes got when she stood on a bridge and looked down into the water below, that told her to go ahead and jump. *Go ahead*, the same feeling told her now. *Let the magic take you.*

Above her, Simi was circling back – her curved hoopoe beak and crest so strangely black.

Was this it, then? Was she destined to become a part of the magic she had fought for the past year and more? The magic that had claimed her parents' lives, and was minutes away from claiming her grandfather's? She sank on to her knees. She had sacrificed the travel world for him, but it had all been in vain because of Neon's lie. How could she have been so naive? *Let the snake come and swallow me.*

Something flashed at the periphery of her vision. Looking up, she saw that the magical barrier had collapsed. Professor Nigm, steady on his feet now, looked down at her with bitter determination. One step behind him stood the rest of the locksmiths, the professors and their apprentices, in formation. Behind them were the Night Folk. Aliya's heart leapt as she recognized Mr Kamel. There were the mythicals she had met at the Grizzled Hen, the baebue, the ghouls and the sila, her thundercloud hanging above her, dark and crackling – a contained storm. Beyond stood the security robots, expressionless and waiting for a command. Inspector Prickly hovered above, his whistle between his teeth. At the sight of them, Aliya's heart was caught between joy and dread. Which side did she belong with now?

They all stood waiting for something. Aliya saw that Nigm's hand was raised, ready to give the command to attack. His pipe smoke was black now, curling around him, creeping up his arm.

The Darkling was almost upon her, so she ran, heading for her mentor. As she passed the Shop's door they began pouring out: pots, pans, hat stands, lamps, rocking chairs . . . a vomit of junk spilt out of the gaping doorway and formed into larger shapes – creatures with big heads and frying-pan hands, giants with steak knives for claws and big metal rubbish bins for forearms. The Shop had geared up for battle. Its doorway was so close that Aliya felt the magic sucking her in.

'You!' Professor Nigm was looking right at her. Aliya hesitated. Behind her, she heard the Darkling coming, its great head rushing over the ground, the whip-crack of its forked tongue.

Professor Nigm lunged towards her, slicing the air open as he came. A portal opened in the air, and with a tug and a shove he sent her through it, closing it behind her just as quickly with a flick of his hand. The last thing Aliya saw was the black scales of the Darkling rushing past as it crashed into the locksmiths and the Night Folk.

She was standing in a desert. It was night and a full moon hung in the sky, a perfect glowing disc. Dunes of silver sand stretched out on all sides, a billowing landscape at once quiet and alive, the sand rippling softly around her feet in its own infinite dance with the wind.

'Where am I?' she spoke out loud, then searched the sky and the sand for the portal Nigm had opened. Could it still be there somewhere? But no. There was no trace of it. He had hurled her out of harm's way. That was clear. At least that meant he still cared for her, didn't it? Even though she had done the unspeakable.

She began walking. Perhaps it wasn't the wisest thing to do, but her body was on fire with anguish and moving gave some relief. As she walked, she noticed that there was a scent of roses on the wind. It was the kind of smell that gave the heart wings, and despite her despair she felt her spirits lift.

Climbing a dune, she caught sight of a cluster of shadows in the distance. Trees and bushes. There was a garden in the desert. As she neared, she heard running water. Stumbling down the last dune, she came to a stop on the shore of a beautiful moonlit lake – an oasis. Tall palm trees with graceful trunks swayed in the breeze, their leafy crowns rustling, rippling silver.

So much stillness and beauty after the evil she had seen. It flooded her senses and she stood drinking in the scene, greedy for its comfort. Someone was sitting by the shore on the other side – the figure of a man. The moonlight shone on his hair, colouring its white into silver. When Aliya recognized who it was, she plunged into the lake, oblivious that the water came up to her waist.

'Geddo,' she panted, pushing on, using her arms to propel herself forward. The water seemed to conspire to carry her onwards. Still, when she reached the other side, she collapsed into the sand. Her grandfather walked down from where he was sitting on a fallen palm trunk to help her up. He wrapped her in a piece of white cloth he had been wearing around his torso, then led her to the palm trunk.

'You're all right?' Aliya asked, looking him over, her eyes searching his bare upper body for the stab wound, but there was nothing there now.

'Of course I am,' Geddo said. 'And so are you, if you just calm down a little and think.'

Aliya shook her head.

'I did something terrible.' She looked back over the oasis from where she had come. The idea of going back seemed impossible. Yet still more impossible was the thought of leaving the Infinitum to crumble at the mercy of the Shop.

'What is this place?' she asked her grandfather. The rose smell was stronger here, and she realized that a garden was stretching out around them in the dark.

'A pocket of time, of mercy, as mysterious as God's grace is infinite. But it's only a place to pass through.' He smiled, and for once it was not a weary smile, but kind and full of peace.

'How could Professor Nigm send me here?'

'I asked him to,' Geddo said. 'I needed to meet you before I go. Sometimes, when someone is on their way, a small pocket of time is created. We both accessed it, you and I, with his help. As elder locksmith, he has that power.'

'Wherever it is you're going, you've got to take me with you,' Aliya said. She leant her head against her grandfather's arm, suddenly overcome with the tiredness that had been accumulating throughout the past days.

'Of course you will come,' Geddo said. 'Everyone must travel this way sooner or later. We will see each other again.' He laid his large hand on the side of her face, almost covering her eyes. 'There is no real separation, only pauses. That's why parting is possible without the heart breaking . . . not irreparably, anyway.'

Aliya, who was catching on, began to resist. The idea rushed through her body, her mind, until every part of her had absorbed what he was saying. Geddo was leaving her for ever.

'Don't say for ever,' Geddo said, as though he had heard her relentless, unforgiving thought. 'Remember this place . . . the moon, the desert, the roses. Remember there are other worlds and states of being. Death is like a door you pass through on your way to a new life, the real life.'

'I'll be dead without you,' she said dramatically.

'You must choose to live, and to believe. You did nothing wrong.'

'But Simi . . .' Her voice faded. She didn't know how to tell Geddo about what had happened to her and her nadim. How Simi had turned black and how drawn they both were to the Darkling. But she found she couldn't hold back. She told him everything.

'There's a mystery there,' Geddo said when she had finished. 'I spent so much of my life letting guilt dictate my actions. Don't be like me. You're a wonderful, brave girl, and I love you. You'll be all right.'

He gently enfolded her in his arms. As he did, the scene around her melted away – Geddo and his embrace, the desert, the smell of roses – until she was sitting in an alley on the edge of Qahira Square. In front of her, the battle was raging. Aliya could see the sky over the square light up with flashes of magic, and hear a crackling like thunder. She heard Prickly's whistle too, bursting out commands to the robots, and wondered about Victoria, hoping she was all right. With a stab of worry, she remembered her friends. Where were they? Were they there too, fighting?

Geddo, who had always tried to keep her far from harm's way, had sent her back to the war. *That* was truly mysterious. For a moment, all she wanted to do was sit and cry, but then she recalled what Geddo had said. Their separation wasn't for ever. It was just a pause. She would remember the moonlit desert, and that unearthly smell of roses, and she would grieve, but not now. Not when the sky of the world she loved was coming apart and the ground was cracking to pieces and her friends were at risk.

She had done nothing wrong, Geddo had said. Standing silently, watching the battle unfold, Aliya went back in her mind to the beginning, to when Simi had begun growing that patch of black, to the moments when they had opened portals to find the Darkling waiting for them . . . to the strange longing she felt when she looked at the black snake. There was a mystery there. How would she unravel it? This was the question her mind asked, yet somehow, she felt the answer unfolding inside her like a blooming rose.

Chapter 19
THE BRIGHTLING

She walked towards the square. In front of her, Night Folk on carpets were battling with monsters made of cursed objects, and with other things that must have sprung out of the Shop while she was away – demons with red eyes and bodies like shadows; nasnas, who resembled bald, skinny humans but whose bodies were stunted, and who were hopping along with only one leg and one arm. There were other dark beings too, vicious types of djinn, some in animal form, others red, blue or black, horrific and quick.

Some of the Night Folk looked just as frightening as their enemies. There were water genies and sirens, their faces greenish and pale, their eyes like black pools, their hair dripping with water. There were trolls and wildermen with grimy beards and wooden clubs. There were ghouls and silas, whipping up thunder and lightning.

She knew whose side they were on only by the position they held, protecting the locksmiths who, standing in formation, were working to hold the world together. She could see Professor Nigm's smoke billowing over the rifts in the sky, too many to count now. The other locksmiths, Janus Quartz and Marmaduke Bunting, Aina AbdelRaqib and Mahmoud Ghorab, were struggling, using the powers channelled through their nadims, to heal the rifts and close the cracks that ran through the ground and sky. But even from a distance, Aliya could tell that they were losing. The Shop was swelling, getting ever bigger and blacker, spawning more windows and turrets, eating up the square, forcing the departments around it to crash and crumble.

Aliya closed her eyes and lifted her hands. If she let her mind take over, there would be nothing but fear and despair. She would freeze again, like before, and not be a part of at least trying to save this world. But she could do nothing without her nadim. Where *was* she? When Aliya had been thrust into the time pocket by Nigm, Simi had been left behind. Aliya scanned the blackened sky, trying to discern the shape of a black bird, but it was no use. She would have to try another way.

Come to me. Without opening her eyes, she knew her hands were lighting up, bursting with the colours of the Sublimes. *Come to me*, she called to Simi.

Moments passed and then . . . she felt the nadim coming. And when she opened her eyes, what she saw made her gasp. Simi was not alone. With her was the Darkling, slithering towards her along the narrow alley. Simi had alighted on its head. Now, she lowered her wings as if to say, *Don't be afraid*.

And there was nowhere to run. Aliya glanced back over her shoulder. She could try, but it would be no use. She had let the Darkling come so close that a simple forward lunge would clamp her between its jaws. But running was not the answer. She had to stay. She had to do what Simi had known they must do all along – a knowledge Aliya's heart had known, but that her mind had resisted.

Reaching her, the giant snake stopped and laid its head down on the ground.

Remember, it whispered in her heart. *Remember and release me*. It was the same command, Aliya realized, that the Darkling had uttered every time they had met. In the Smithy, on board the *Silver Express* – the snake had always asked the same thing. *Release me*. But she hadn't understood what it meant, until now.

Taking a step forward, Aliya laid her glowing hands on the Darkling's snout. At once, a memory rose within her, as clear as if she were seeing it with open eyes. She was in her mother's workshop, flying around the room, astride a golden dragon. Her mum was below, laughing up at her.

'You were my mother's nadim,' she told the Darkling. '*She* made you. She forged you with her skill and her love and poured her soul into you, and it's still there – her soul. I can feel it. Then Dorian forced his magic on you. He stole you and made you a slave. That's what turned you black.'

The Darkling shuddered under her hands.

Thank you, it said.

Opening her eyes, she saw the black scales on the Darkling's body fall away. A bright, golden sheen was peeking through from underneath. The enormous body rippled, shedding the blackness and exploding in a symphony of gold and silver scales. Now Simi began to change too. Dissolving, she became a mass of golden liquid that divided into two streams on top of the Darkling's head, then seeped into the empty eye sockets, reforming into two proper eyes. Simi had returned to her original state. She had again become the Darkling's gold, glowing eyes – a part of her mother's nadim. That was why Simi had stayed with Aliya, first as a sparkling grain, then as a nadim of sorts, but never quite at peace. Simi had recognized Aliya's kinship to her mother, her original owner. Her turning black must have been her way of signalling to Aliya where she belonged – that she was part of the Darkling and needed to return. *That was why the key whisperer told me she was homesick*, Aliya thought, remembering her peculiar encounter with the old genie back at the Smithy.

We are whole once more, the Darkling said. *And yours to command.*

Aliya traced her hand along the back of the golden creature, feeling the energy pulsing pure and holy within it. But it wasn't a snake any longer. A mane, like fire, crowned its neck and a pair of magnificent wings lay along its side. It had grown massive, muscular legs.

'You're a dragon!' Aliya exclaimed. Overcome, she hugged it, feeling closer to her mother than ever before.

'And you're not a Darkling any more,' she whispered to the nadim. 'You're a *Brightling*.'

Climbing on to the Brightling's back, Aliya felt the enormous power it contained. It had been feeding directly from the Sublimes and now that the magic was gone, the power was clean and potent.

'Come on!' she cried. 'Let's fly!'

Spreading its wings, the Brightling rose up through the narrow alley and over the rooftops, where Aliya steered it in a large swoop. They headed straight for the Shop. As soon as they were near enough, the Brightling opened its glittering jaws wide and roared. A cascade of brightness burst out, a flood of Baraka energy that, when it touched the Shop's roof, melted part of it away into nothingness.

'Yeah!' Aliya cried, easing her hold on the Brightling's mane and punching the sky. Maybe this was why the Sublimes hadn't resisted the Darkling – they had fed its power, knowing that it would once again become this magnificent magic-fighting weapon. That was why the Smithy had allowed them to reach and pass through the silver door, and into the cave where the Sublimes resided. This was why Simi had told her everything would be all right. It had been a ruse all along!

Aliya and the Brightling swerved and came back, each time battering the Shop with floods of Baraka, melting its turrets and tiles, obliterating its towers and windows. Zooming over the square, they let Baraka fall like rain which, as it touched the demons and ifrits, set them on fire. They collapsed, melting and screaming, until nothing was left but charred remains.

They continued unceasingly, until there was nothing left of the Shop but the doorway, which finally collapsed with a great crack on to the cobblestones.

Then a great roar went up from the Night Folk and the travellers who had approached to watch the undoing of magic. The robots roared too, as Prickly and Victoria, still on their carpets, soot-stained, exhausted but triumphant, blew their whistles above them.

As Aliya landed with the Brightling, the crowd gathered around. There was relief and triumph, but grief too, for the ones lost. Aliya could see them lying strewn across the square, being tended to by the survivors.

Reminded of her own lost friends, her chest surged with new fear. Stepping up on the Brightling's back, she cupped her hands and shouted for them.

'Here!' Karima was pressing through the crowd, her face flushed. Aliya could see she was cradling her arm, and that she was bleeding from a cut on her forehead. Reaching down, Aliya helped her climb up next to her.

'Here!' Fuad came towards them, carried on the sea of people, unharmed but looking as though he had rolled in mud and jumped through fire. Then came Mustafa, riding on the back of a flying hieracosphinx who hovered close enough for him to jump across to the Brightling's back.

'I carried one of their youngsters to safety during the fight,' he called out. The hieracosphinx gave an ear-splitting caw and Mustafa cowered. 'I don't speak hieraco well, but I think he said that he's given me his trust . . . or that he'll grind me to mush.'

'Where's Aion?' Aliya asked, looking around. Then she saw her, carried on the arms and hands of the travellers beneath them. She was unconscious, but breathing. She was hauled on to the Brightling's back; her face was smeared with dirt, her striped hair tousled. She was wearing her smartsuit, which flickered in and out of invisibility mode, making her flash in and out of view.

'We found her lying there,' a bulky sphinx called, pointing to where the Smithy's golden doorway still stood. The locksmiths had sealed it closed again, and the door shone bright. The red letters that had spelt 'traitors' were gone.

'Let me look at her.' Karima sat on her knees next to Aion. 'She's had some sort of shock,' she concluded after examining her. 'Let me try this.'

Fishing a vial out of the medicine belt she wore slung around her torso, she dripped a few drops into Aion's mouth. They waited with bated breath.

'Come on,' Karima muttered through clenched teeth. 'Nereid spit always works. It always does.'

And so it did. Soon Aion coughed, then opened her eyes.

Everyone exhaled in relief. Fuad wiped his wet eyes.

'To the sanatorium, everybody,' a stern voice rang out. It was Inspector Prickly, hovering next to them on a carpet. 'You all need to be tended to, even if you think you are all right.'

'I'll take them, Papa,' Victoria said, waving at the pod.

Prickly saluted his daughter, then turned his carpet around and swept away over the square, a troop of robots following him in a rapid trot. There would still be Loopers to track down and arrest. Leaping from the Brightling's back, Aliya landed next to Victoria on the battered carpet and squeezed her in a hug.

'Were you really going to join the Loopers?' Aliya asked her.

'Of course not,' Victoria said. 'It takes more than some bumbling idiots in hoods to crack a Prickly.'

Aliya, realizing the carpet itself was no stranger, fell on her knees.

'Marauder, old boy.' Aliya rubbed the Persian across his patterns and his fringe.

The carpet curled up its edges in happiness, until Victoria screamed that she was falling off. Then, bruised and laughing and crying by turn, the friends joined the procession of survivors towards the sanatorium to rest and heal just like the inspector had ordered. The Brightling carried some of them, her great golden body moving through the streets ahead of the crowd like a beacon of hope.

Chapter 20

SOMETHING OTHER THAN CAMEL FEET

At the sanatorium, the pod was separated by brisk nurses who put the boys and the girls in different rooms. But once the children had been examined and cleaned and had a good sleep, they gathered in the girls' room, which was bright and spacious, its windows tickled by the green crowns of the mango trees that grew in the square outside. Mrs Dickens, ruddy, dusted with flour and still in her apron with the sunflower print, was the first visitor to arrive. With her was a host of ghoul maids carrying baskets of breakfast food. The cook and her helpers had been put under house arrest by the Loopers, and had distracted themselves from the horror of what was happening in the city outside by cooking. Good food, Mrs Dickens breathlessly told them as she unpacked the many delights from her basket, was essential to the children's recovery. They had to be good children and eat it all up. The pod didn't disagree.

Once Mrs Dickens had left, the friends sat for a long time at the small table. They had a lot to talk about. First, they went through all the events that had occurred in detail, each one recounting his or her version of events. They spoke about how they had been separated in the hall of mirrors. While Mustafa and Aliya had managed to escape with the help of Hafiza, the rest of them had been rounded up by the mythicals who served the Loopers.

'That was when I decided to go undercover,' Victoria told them, the only one in the pod the Loopers had asked to join them. 'They were right in noticing my natural superiority – that's obviously why they offered me the chance to join – but were wrong to think that I would betray my pod.'

When it was Aliya's turn to speak, she looked at Karima.

'When I was lost in the space-time glitch and

floating among the stars, I thought I saw you.' She looked down at her knotted fingers. 'I know you did your best for Geddo. I shouldn't have doubted that. You're the kind of person who always does her best for people. You always have been.'

Karima reached across the table and squeezed Aliya's hand. Squeezing back, Aliya looked around at the others, feeling grateful. She'd only ever had these friends, the ones that sat gathered here at this table, smiling at her. They had made her feel part of something – something that mattered.

'I forgot to tell you who helped Papa and me vitalize the robots, to make them easier to control . . . like the carpets,' Victoria said, interrupting Aliya's thoughts. 'It was your mentor, Professor Nigm.'

Aliya looked at her in surprise.

'We kept it under wraps,' Victoria continued, a little smugly. 'That's the policy when it's a security issue.'

Aliya thought of the secret project Nigm had been busy with at the Smithy. His rushing off, the closed doors. During the whirlwind of accusations against the locksmiths, it had made her suspect that even he was up to something bad. *So, was this it?* Did that mean her mentor was free of guilt? She was almost sure, but a sliver of doubt still lived in her heart. What did that smoky memory of him doing magic truly mean?

When things had more or less returned to normal and they were sitting in the professor's private workshop one afternoon after the day's practice, it was Nigm who, quite out of the blue, brought it up. Aliya was polishing instruments. She had lined them up in a beautiful row, each one ready to be tucked into their special place in the toolbelt the locksmiths used when working on travel keys. The professor was reclining in his armchair over in the cosy corner where the fireplace was, smoking his pipe and looking thoughtfully into the flames. As the lilac smoke wandered upwards, it took on shapes that dissolved as soon as they touched the ceiling. Several times, Aliya had caught sight of the smoky resemblance of herself, and of Geddo. The professor was thinking about her, and of her late grandfather. Worrying, no doubt, and wondering if she was all right. She'd never thought he'd be such a worrier. But then again, he had lost loved ones too, and knew the pain of grief as keenly as she did.

Aliya tucked the last silver instrument into its pocket. It had been three months since Geddo passed away. They had buried him in the Muslim graveyard back in Cairo on a crisp morning. Her friends had all been there, as had Geddo's old colleagues from the Brigade, Great-Aunt Gigi and Esmat. Even some of the Night Folk had attended in disguise. Since then, everyone had treated her as if she were an egg that might break if squeezed too hard.

Yes, the sadness was there, thudding softly in her chest, and she missed him. Geddo had been her family, had cared for her since she was a wee thing, had done his best to feed her, to brush her hair, to teach her manners. He was gone and it hurt.

But she was all right. She was all right because she remembered the moonlit desert where they had said goodbye. If she concentrated, she could still feel the rose scent in her nose, filling her with something unearthly and peaceful. Death was not the end. It was a pause. She would see Geddo again, when she was finished living in the world. Death was like stepping through a door, like going from one room into another.

Through the window, Aliya could see the Brightling asleep in the corridor outside. She was pretty much obstructing the path, and several times that afternoon locksmiths had been forced to climb over her to get past. Her size was a bit of a problem, but only when they were indoors. It was a different thing altogether when they soared the skies of the Infinitum. That morning, Aliya had taken her for a ride, and they'd circled the city in a wild swoop, the Brightling lighting up the sky like a firework. She'd absorbed so much Sublime energy that she still glowed, which was why none of the locksmiths complained about her, even as she made them clamber over her glittering scales and muscular legs, even when they got slapped by one of her great wings as she stretched them in her sleep. Aliya's only trouble these days was getting the Brightling to transform into a key shape. It hadn't happened yet, and there was no telling if it ever would. Nigm had said, 'That much Baraka needs a dragon to carry it.' In essence, they would just have to wait and see. In the meantime, he had made her a new travel key, with a blade shaped like a golden dragon's head.

As Aliya rolled the instruments up in their leather cover, she felt her stomach growl. She had already nipped over to the mantelpiece where the professor's cookie jar stood, to help herself to petits fours and chocolate sablés (the professor didn't mind), but now it was almost dinner time, and she was ravenous.

'I suppose you are wondering about the jar?' Nigm said, as Aliya began gathering her things. 'The one with the skull on it?'

Aliya stopped what she was doing to look at him. She had tiptoed around her mentor for weeks, waiting for the right moment to ask him about the jar, but had been unable to rally the courage. Since the showdown with the Loopers, Nigm had been more reticent than ever, which meant she hardly got a word out of him. Aliya no longer suspected him of being up to anything bad. He had saved her life, after all, and fought against the Loopers. Still, the issue was unexplained, and it bothered her.

She watched as Nigm walked over and pulled the jar off the shelf where it had stood for the last few weeks, looming over them. He had not bothered to hide it. Rather, he had placed it in a prominent spot.

As he uncorked it, the workshop grew darker, just as Neon's office had when he'd opened it. There it was again: the image of the professor doing magic unfurled in the air between them.

'It was after I lost my wife and daughter in the earthquake,' Nigm said, his voice rusty from lack of use. 'I didn't know how to let them go. I got desperate.'

Aliya gazed at the young man made up of smoke as he pricked his finger. A drop of blood fell on to the desk where he sat. It began to metamorphose into a head. A figure grew out of the blood . . . a neck, shoulders. It continued growing until a man stood on top of the desk. But what Aliya had imagined would become a black, horrific demon turned into the likeness of a bearded old man in a cape and a turban. At the sight of him, the young Nigm burst into tears.

'Who was that?' Aliya asked when her mentor had recalled the smoke by tapping the cork on the neck of the jar.

'My mentor, Soliman Nahhas. He sensed my desperation and watched over me. He was half-genie, so could put on that show you saw. He prevented the magic I tried to summon and came to my rescue. He put me straight. Oh, the scolding I got that day.' He smiled faintly. 'The temptations of magic that you've been faced with were present then as well, and I was young and inexperienced. Certain times in our lives make us more vulnerable. That's why we need to travel through life in packs, like wolves, making sure no one gets left behind. I keep that jar on my shelf always to remind myself of my own weakness. It's an attempt to stay humble, to keep me on my toes.'

Aliya's eyes lingered on the jar in his hands. It was strange to imagine that Professor Nigm too had made a mistake like that – that he had been tempted, just like her, and had found it near impossible to let go of those he loved. But *his* mentor had interfered and saved him, in the nick of time, just like Nigm had saved her. In the midst of the battle in Qahira Square, in her weakest moment, when she thought she might let herself get sucked into the Shop, he had been there. He'd opened a pocket in time and pushed her through. He had saved her from magic which, in essence, meant he had saved her life.

Dorian had told her that she was 'just like' him, and it was both true and false. They had been alike in weakness, in loss and confusion. But, for whatever reasons, he had chosen magic. Maybe things would have been different if he, like her, had travelled in a pack.

'Thanks,' she said, the only word she could think of. Nigm nodded once. He understood and there was no need for more words. 'Now, what about dinner?'

'Yes,' Nigm said, placing the jar back on its shelf. 'It's high time.'

They usually had dinner together on the days she had apprentice duties. Walking over to the unattached door that stood in the portal practice area, Aliya whipped out her new key and felt it grow warm in her hands. She could open portals that actually led where she wanted them to now.

'What do you feel like today?' Aliya asked when they were both standing by the doorway.

When she and Nigm dined together, they usually went back to the 1940s, to one of Cairo's street-food joints, to eat one of Egypt's signature dishes. Aliya preferred koshary, a mix of rice and lentils topped with macaroni, fried onion and spicy tomato sauce. The professor was partial to hawashy – crispy flatbread loaves filled with mincemeat. In the forties they served bigger portions, for a fraction of the price she was used to in her own time. For a few piastre, they could have two heaped portions each *and* rice pudding at the end.

'Why don't I open the portal today?' Nigm said. He hadn't exchanged his turban for a red tarboosh, the way he usually did when they went to that particular time. He took a puff on his pipe, then tapped it on the lock of the door. Aliya gave him an admiring glance. Nigm was so skilled at opening portals that a simple tap was enough to get him where he wanted to go. There was a brief pulse of light from behind the door.

'Not camel feet again.' Aliya gave him a suspicious

look. 'I don't care if they're good for me. They're *disgusting*.'

'Don't you care about your growing bones?' Nigm looked at her, brows raised.

'Uhh, *no*! You know you don't have to worry about me, right?' she added as an afterthought. 'I'm all right. I really am.'

Nigm nodded slowly.

'Still, if you don't mind, I'll make it my business to worry about you. As will Mr Kamel, and your great-aunt and the rest of your friends here in the travel world.'

'All right.' Looking at her feet, Aliya smiled. She shrugged. 'I don't mind.'

Grabbing the handle, she pulled the door open. A rush of air lifted the hair off her shoulders. Below them, the Citadel spread out in all its patchwork glory – a puzzle of housetops and pyramids, temples and towers. There, in mid-air, were her friends, seated on Marauder. In their midst was a large wicker basket, so heavy with food that the carpet slumped in the middle.

'Why don't you join your friends for a picnic

today?' Nigm said. 'Your nadim needs all the exercise she can get.'

He pointed his pipe at the Brightling, who just then let loose a resounding fart. Omar Sadik, who had been passing her in the corridor, cowered in disgust.

Aliya smiled. At the sound of her call, the Brightling woke up and bounded across the workshop to join her, nearly getting stuck in the doorway on the way out. With Nigm's help, Aliya hauled herself on to the golden dragon's back. With Aliya clinging to her fiery mane, they shot into the air and past Marauder, who immediately took up the chase. Aliya turned to wave goodbye to Nigm, but then remembered that the portals leading to the Smithy were always opaque from the outside. She waved anyway, knowing he could see her.

They swooped down, skimming the housetops, then shot back up into the clouds. Spring was in the air. Aliya could smell it – a freshness of flowering trees carried on the wind.

In places where rifts were still visible, Aliya slowed the Brightling to a hover, and the dragon breathed her luminous breath, healing the cracks. Just like the sky, the city was healing. The Night Folk, together with the senior locksmiths, had managed to recover all the seniors from the remnants of the Shop. Salman Bashiri and the others had been retrieved by a special Night Folk unit who had raided the Loopers' HQ to find a whole lot of victims, including the Ghoulies. Last Aliya heard, Salman was back to his old boisterous self, but still under supervision at the sanatorium, along with his podmates. After his time in the hall of mirrors, he would have to be re-evaluated by the Reform and Civilization committee before he returned to his studies.

The enslaved mythicals had been set free from their metaphysical bonds, and the Loopers had been rounded up by Prickly's robots, at least those whom Infinitum Security had been able to identify. It was likely more were still on the run, or even hiding in plain sight. Those who had been caught were now imprisoned, including Arsinoe. Aliya had not seen her since the events at Qahira Square, and she wouldn't mind never clapping eyes on her again.

People who thought of themselves as superior to others really didn't belong in this world, or any other that she knew of.

When they'd had their fill of flying, the pod rested on the roof of the Travel Inventions Department, one of the only buildings that had remained unscathed during the battle with the Shop. There they explored the contents of Mrs Dickens's hamper, and found that she had outdone herself yet again. There was a thermos with hot chocolate, a jar of whipped cream, shortbread, jam cookies, rock cakes, gingersnaps and baguette sandwiches stuffed with brie and turkey.

Below them, life in Qahira Square was returning to normal. The traces of the Shop had been cleaned away, and the buildings that had been damaged were scaffolded and being rebuilt.

'Are you going to wear that all the time?' Aliya asked Victoria when they had finished eating and sat sipping cordial, leaning their backs against the Brightling, who was snoozing in the last rays of the sun. She pointed at the crest and star medal that was pinned to the lapel of Victoria's jacket. Their whole pod had received the Khedivial Badge of Honour for their role in locating the lost locksmiths, but only Victoria wore it on every outfit. Great-Aunt Gigi had tried to make Aliya do the same, but she had refused. They had agreed, though, that Aliya would wear it on special occasions.

'It's there to remind Papa what I'm worth, in case he forgets,' Victoria said, tapping her badge. She smiled into the setting sun. 'Although I'm starting to think he knows already. He even let me keep this.' She fished out a whistle.

'Our mum framed our medals and hung them in the living room,' Karima said. She laid an arm around her brother's neck. 'She's not threatened to bring us home once since the Shop was beaten. It's heaven!'

'She nearly lost the plot when we told her about the hall of mirrors,' Fuad said, grinning. 'But she'll have to get used to stuff like that happening now that we're on the fast-track to becoming real travellers.'

'The hieracosphinx guard has made me an honorary member,' Mustafa said with a smile. 'That kind of trumped the medal for me, although that was also nice, of course. Dad was proud. That thing about grinding me to mush was just me getting some *caws* mixed up.'

'My family's going to screen-free camp this summer,' Aion said. 'I think learning about Neon's uber-tech dystopia got them thinking about their own lifestyle choices.'

'I guess we showed them,' Victoria said.

'I guess we did,' Aliya added.

Then they fell silent and watched the sun set, knowing that the world they loved was safe once more, and that they had been part of making it so. And that was, for their young hearts, no small thing to savour.

ACKNOWLEDGEMENTS

My gratitude and thanks to:

You, dear reader, for coming along with Aliya and her friends all the way to the end of this series. I hope you've enjoyed reading it as much as I have enjoyed writing it.

Barry Cunningham, for sticking it out with me and never telling me to reduce my word count. In these times of budget cuts and gloomy reading statistics, that means a lot.

Laura Myers, and the rest of the Chicken House team and Scholastic UK. It's been a true pleasure working with you all. I hope it's not the last time.

Lucy Irvine, for her good advice in uncertain times. An agent in need is an agent indeed.

Rachel Hickman, Gaia Alessi and Helen Crawford-White, for yet another great, vibrant cover.

Fraser Crichton and Jenny Glencross, for your eagle-eyed editing skills.

Claudia Feldmann, for taking time out of a busy schedule to help me look for loopholes.

The 2024 Debut Buddies, without whom writing would have been a very lonely occupation.

Matthew Fox, for his insights into the mysterious world of publishing.

To my mother, who shares my love of reading and who, despite her limited English, insists on reading everything I write.

To my children, yalla! Learn from Grandma!